EVERY PERFECT GIFT

JULIE NYE

Bob Jones University Press, Greenville, South Carolina 29614

Every Perfect Gift

Edited by Carla Vogt

Cover by Cheryl Weikel

To the two people who have influenced my writing
more than any others:

Dr. Ray St. John,
who taught by example and with tremendous perception—
and who never stopped asking "What if?"

and

Bob Whitmore,
who spent years being a great boss,
a patient tutor, and a good friend

Books by Julie Nye

In My Uncle's House
Scout
Every Perfect Gift

Publisher's Note

Sherri James has a dream, but she's afraid that it is too far beyond the realm of her life on a Montana cattle ranch. How can she ever make her father understand her desire to be an artist? And how can she know whether she's on the right track?

When Sherri prays, asking for God's help, she isn't prepared to get an answer that includes an unwanted stepmother. Through deepening conflicts with a woman who is different from herself, she begins to realize that God has more for her to learn than technique in the field of art.

A series of unusual circumstances and a close brush with death help her to understand that the Lord often answers prayer and meets needs in ways that are far better than anything she could ever have imagined. As the story unfolds, Sherri finds herself with an exciting opportunity to realize her dream. But before she can make the most of it, she must come to terms with her stepmother in the way that God intended.

*"Every good gift and every perfect gift is from above,
and cometh down from the Father of lights,
with whom is no variableness, neither shadow of turning."*
James 1:17

Chapter One

Snowdrifts sparkled in the glow from the setting sun as Sherri stepped off the last rural-route afternoon bus. A blast of subzero January wind made her gasp and draw her scarf higher up around her face. While the bus chugged away with its gears groaning and whining, Sherri started toward the ranch gate.

She took a tighter grasp on her schoolbooks and quickened her pace. She didn't need to look at her watch to know that she was awfully late. Her brothers would have been home nearly two hours ago, and at this rate supper would undoubtedly be far behind schedule. All she could do was hope that something would delay her father in getting to the house this evening.

But as she neared the gate at the head of the long driveway, she saw a heavily bundled form pushing its way through the new drifts to meet her. Beside the bundle came a German shepherd, belly-deep in snow.

"Sherri!" A voice reached her. "Sherri! Hurry up!"

The shepherd left his companion and came running ahead, leaping waist-high with delight. "Hi, Dash." She freed a hand to pat his head.

"Sherri! Come on! You've got to hurry!"

"What's wrong, Timmy?" Sherri asked as she neared him. Between his hat and his scarf, all she could see of the seven-year-old's face was his eyes—and they looked worried.

"Boy, are you in trouble!" White gusts came from beneath his muffler as he gasped out the words. "We've got company coming for supper, and Mrs. Andersen went home early 'cause she was sick, and Dad just came in and found out nothing's done and you weren't home."

"Oh, no." Sherri groaned, starting for the house in the middle of her little brother's last sentence. "Company! Who?"

"I don't know. He didn't tell us."

She repeated the groan and attempted to turn her fast walk into a run, despite the knee-deep snow. The driveway of Rockview Ranch had never seemed this long before. By the time she neared the door, Timmy was far behind. Her lungs ached and her throat burned from the cold and exertion.

She took a brief moment to knock the snow from her boots before entering the front door. Dropping her school books on the hall table, she shed her coat and boots in nearly the same move. Perspiration dampened the hair around her face. She tumbled her wraps into the closet, picked up her books again, and started down the hall toward the kitchen.

"Sheryl Renee James." She heard her father's voice. Sherri paused and took a breath before she turned around. He was standing in his office doorway, just to the left of the front door.

"Sir?"

"I suspect you may have noticed that it's after five o'clock?"

"Yes, sir."

"More than two hours after the time you are due home from school?"

"Yes, sir."

There was a long silence. It grew longer and longer as Sherri tried not to fidget under his stare. Then he surprised her by exhaling a long sigh, as though he didn't feel up to the effort of the discussion. "Sherri, we have four people coming for dinner in less than an hour. The kitchen is a federal disaster area, and nothing has even been started for supper."

Sherri clenched her hands. What a treat.

"Mrs. Andersen took some steaks from the freezer this morning, but nothing else has been done. I had Kyle start the charcoal a few minutes ago."

"What else do you want fixed?"

"I don't know. Whatever." He turned back into his office. Sherri stared after him, perplexed. She wondered whether he was feeling well, but she didn't waste much time puzzling about it.

Hurrying to the kitchen, Sherri slung her things onto the counter and went to the sink to wash her hands. It took her a moment to realize that her brother, Kyle, was under the table, swiping at something with a dishcloth.

"What are you doing?" She paused, holding the towel in front of her.

"Destroying evidence. I hope." His voice sounded resigned. Kyle hardly ever got upset at anything. "This," he continued, crawling out from under the table, "is what's left of Mrs. Andersen's pottery urn that used to sit over there." He gestured at the counter with a large blue shard. "No one's admitted responsibility yet, but Todd is a likely guess."

"Anyway," he continued without giving her time to break in, "Dad hasn't said who's coming to dinner, but it seems to be the event of the month. So, if you'll tell me what to do, maybe I can help you get the show on the road—ya' know? Dad's a little hot about you being late."

"I know, I know." Sherri slung the towel back over the towel bar. "Okay, go downstairs and find me some good, *big* potatoes. No soft spots, no sprouts. We'll have baked potatoes with the steak. Then maybe some mixed vegetables? A tossed salad might be better—better but not quicker." Sherri continued thinking out loud, but Kyle had already headed downstairs.

He was the best thing in brothers that had ever been invented, Sherri thought. Of the five brothers that she had,

Kyle was closest to her in age. They'd learned early to stick together.

Their family was the fourth generation of Jameses that had lived on the sprawling Rockview Ranch in Montana. Paul and Debbie James had continued family tradition here with their own six children, until a blood clot claimed Debbie's life when their youngest, Tim, was three days old. Sherri was eight years old then.

Now Tim was seven; Todd, eight; Kyle, thirteen; and Sherri, fifteen. Shane would graduate from high school in the spring, and Terry, the oldest, was two years through a degree in electronics engineering at a local college.

Sherri flew around the kitchen, thankful for the millionth time for the microwave oven. When Kyle reappeared with the potatoes, she was frantically chopping lettuce to add to the nearby stack of tomatoes, carrots, peppers, and celery. "Good," she said, looking them over as he held them out. "Scrub them off and poke some holes in the top with a fork. Then just put them on the counter and see if you can find any cottage cheese in the refrigerator." Sherri began scraping vegetables into a large wooden bowl.

The back door bounced open, and Tim—complete with dog—came charging in with a deluge of snow. "Hey, Sherri! What's for supper? Can I have some—"

"Tim, get the dog out of the house!" The distraction made her dump several tomato "innards" down the front of her sweater. "No, you can't have anything until supper—and get your boots off!"

"Dash is all right! I'll clean the snow up."

"Get him out, Tim. Now!" She swung around and took a step toward him. "Scoot. And you bet you'll clean the snow up. If you're not finished and washed up in five minutes, you can forget supper."

Tim grabbed Dash's collar, pulling the big dog toward the door. He knew when she meant business. Sherri paid no more attention to him for the moment. She grabbed the cottage cheese from Kyle. Popping it open, she began spooning it into little bowls. "You guys put the extra leaf in the table," she said as Tim reappeared minus coat, boots, and dog. "Dig out the dark blue tablecloth and the napkins from the closet. Put the cloth on *straight* and find some rings for the napkins."

They disappeared into the dining room. Sherri kept going, making much better time with no one in the way. Pineapple in the cottage cheese; top it with cherries. Her rushing thoughts were barely keeping time with her hands. Bowls on a tray; tray into the refrigerator. Dishes down from cupboard; glasses; count out the silverware. Check potatoes to make sure they have holes. Salad in refrigerator. Check ice-cream supply in freezer. Pull out parfait glasses and chocolate sauce. Steaks laid out on platter—tenderizer, seasoning. . . . "Kyle! Is the charcoal ready?"

"Should be." He came through the door, pulled on his coat, grabbed the steaks, and disappeared outside. Grilling steaks in the winter might seem a little strange to many people, Sherri realized, but it was a favorite with their father; so he'd constructed a little shelter off the back patio. Far from a perfect situation, it at least kept the snowflakes off the meat, and the wind off the cook, while the charcoal did its work.

Sherri threw a desperate glance at the clock and headed for the dining room with a stack of dishes. Ten minutes later, she snapped the microwave door shut, set the timer, and punched the start button. "Now," she turned to Tim. "Where is Todd? Would you go—no, never mind." She pulled a counter stool in front of the microwave. "You sit right here. Don't budge. When that timer goes off, turn the tray of potatoes around and reset the timer for five more minutes. Don't change the power setting. Got it?"

He nodded, looking a little woebegone. "Thanks." She gave his shoulder a pat, grabbed her school things off the counter, and ran for her room. The ranch house was a large one, but it was all on one level. Being the only girl, Sherri had always enjoyed the advantage of having her own room.

Even though there were two spare rooms, the guys had always had to share.

She checked the living room, the den, the bathrooms, and all the spare bedrooms on the way to her own room—which was at the far end of the house—but no Todd. That kid, she thought. He knows he ought to be around. It's almost supper time anyway.

No time for worrying, though. She glanced at her watch again. Fifteen minutes till zero hour. She made a fast change into the first fresh skirt and blouse she could lay her hands on. Throwing a despairing glance in the mirror, she grabbed a brush. Her hair was sandy blonde and violently curly. The battle was over in moments—she quit and bundled the whole mess into a braid, tying the end with a green ribbon that sort of matched her blouse.

Ten minutes to go. She pushed her feet back into her loafers and did a close check of her face for stray shreds of lettuce. She stepped closer to the mirror, brushing back a loose wisp of hair, looking for a place to tuck it in. In doing so, she drew her own attention to a slightly crumpled sketch of her two little brothers that was stuck near the top of the glass. She paused, then pulled the piece of paper loose and fingered it thoughtfully. In the space of a breath, the impending dinner faded away as her thoughts swept back to the scene she'd witnessed at the mall on the way to the bus stop that afternoon.

A woman was sitting at a makeshift artist's easel, just inside the doorway of the main entrance, busily sketching away at something. A crowd clustered around her. Sherri could hear the exclamations from outside the door. Thinking it would just take a moment, she slipped through the door to try to get a peek at the easel.

When she had a clear view of the artist's work, Sherri's breath caught in her throat at the magnificent portrait that was developing: the face of a young woman who stood motionless before the lady artist. Quickly her portrait took shape, grew hair, and took on the clothing that the girl was wearing. The colors, the hair style, the tilt of the head—it all became lifelike enough to leap off the paper. Then the artist was finished. Money changed hands and another portrait was begun. Bus, home, and all other concerns had left Sherri's mind completely.

"Sherri!" The call jerked her from her recollections.

"Yes, Dad." She flicked off the light and stepped into the hall. "It's almost ready. I just need to check on the last few things."

"Okay. Then come into the living room. I want you to meet our guests."

"Dad?" Sherri stopped him as he turned away.

"Hmm?"

"Have you seen Todd? I can't find him anywhere—"

"Yeah. He was hiding in the barn." Sherri caught a note of amusement in her father's slightly exasperated tone. "I guess he broke something of Mrs. Andersen's and panicked. He's in the living room with everyone else now."

"Is he cleaned up for supper?"

"Good enough. He looks presentable, anyway."

"All right." Sherri followed her father down the hall. "Dad?" The question started out before she could think, or she would have known better. "Do you remember when I asked about drawing lessons last month? Do you think I'll be able—"

"Later, Sherri. This is no time for a discussion. Besides, how can you take on anything else when so much of what you have to do now runs so far behind schedule?"

With that rather pointed remark, her father turned into the hallway that led to the living room. Sherri sighed as she continued toward the kitchen. The main problem with his answer was that one word: *later.* In more than two years of asking, it had never gotten any "later." Sherri didn't figure he was deliberately putting her off. He just didn't think about it much. There were always so many pressing things at the ranch that were demanding his attention.

"Anymore," he was always saying, "if I blink my eyes more than once a day I'm three weeks behind schedule."

It's not all his fault, Sherri reminded herself. You can't expect him to know what you won't tell him.

That was the rest of the problem. Why, she wondered, does it always have to be so hard to talk about things that are so important? Sherri didn't know when her fascination for art had first taken over. She could remember feeling the longing in the dim past when she'd stubbornly tried to make her stubby, five-year-old fingers copy her mother's beautiful drawings and paintings. But Mom was a professional, Sherri told herself as she checked the potatoes and shooed Tim into the living room. She was doing book illustrations for a publishing company when she met Dad. That's a long way beyond my little sketches.

But she could hope. For Sherri, the childish thrill of crayon, pencil, and paper had never quite evaporated. On a bookshelf in her room were several sketch pads that were treasured possessions. Their pages were filled with beautifully detailed sketches. Years and years ago, Sherri had sat and watched in fascination as those sketches developed under her mother's hands as an accompaniment to the long stories she made up.

How in the world do people ever figure out how to get such realism on paper, Sherri wondered. She had labored over her own attempts but kept them carefully concealed from everyone. The few times that others had caught glimpses of her work, their remarks had been complimentary. Like the day her art teacher had caught her trying to draw Taffy, her horse, when the mare had been little more than a gangly filly.

"That's really well done," he'd told her. But Sherri hadn't been able to manage anything more than a scowl. It didn't look much like Taffy to her. As she remembered the perfect detail in the sketches she'd seen at the mall, she sighed. Pausing for a moment at the window in the hall, she tried to collect her nerves a little before greeting the guests. It didn't seem to work. Hands on the window ledge, she leaned her forehead against the frozen coldness of the glass. Darkness had fallen, and a scant half moon was already emerging above the jagged mountain peaks. Everything else was held still and silent beneath the icy grip of the glittering snow.

Sherri's thoughts went on of their own accord, imagining what the artist in the mall would be able to do with a scene like the one before her. A burst of laughter from the next room dragged her attention back to the business at hand. With a sigh, she pushed herself upright and away from the window.

Chapter Two

Sherri remembered her immediately. After one look at the immaculate brunette woman seated on the sofa, Sherri's stomach, already churned up, felt the way it had the time her brothers had filled her Coke can with washing soda. The glow in her father's tone as he began introductions banished the rest of her doubts. Sherri shot a glance at him, thinking of the last place she had seen the lady—at the Larsons' barbeque last fall.

She followed her father's trail of introductions from the woman, whose name was Lynn, to Lynn's parents, Mr. and Mrs. Fallester. But she hadn't noticed the dark-haired girl sitting at the far end of the room, in the corner chair by the fireplace. "This is Kathleen Merriell, Lynn's daughter."

Sherri's face felt hot, and she hoped she didn't look as flushed as she felt. Kathleen was a few years older than Sherri, and she was almost a carbon copy of her mother. Her silky dark hair hadn't a wisp out of place; her clothes were tailored to the stitch. She sat motionless with a beautiful smile and perfect poise.

Sherri wasn't really listening to what her father was saying. Something about their being from Wisconsin—friends of the Larsons; they'd decided to move out here in the spring. Sherri stared at the carpet for a few moments, realizing how many things this explained: her dad's unusual amount of time spent in town recently, the trip East in November, the slightly detached mood at odd times.

Sherri was suddenly very conscious of her thrown-together skirt and top and the scuffed loafers. She took another glance at Kathleen, realizing that compared to her she looked about ten years old—and as though she'd been playing in the back yard all day. Her eyes crept to Lynn Merriell again. To her surprise, Lynn was watching her, too. Her gaze was direct and warm, and seemed as though it had a little bit of a question in it. Sherri's chin went up slightly before she could think about her response.

She was surprised at the stiffness she felt. The lady hadn't even spoken to her yet. But hostility surged up in Sherri just the same. She thought it was probably showing in her eyes, so she finally tore away from the stare down. Taking a step back, she propped a shoulder against the doorjamb and folded her arms in front of her. The only problem now was that she couldn't figure out where to look next. She settled for the arm of the nearest chair, studying its wood-grain pattern as the voices in the room began to register with her again.

"No, way. He can have the computers. I want to get into some kind of a pre-med program, or pre-vet, or whatever you want to call it. Maybe, eventually, we can keep some of the animal-upkeep money in the family. Dad figures that we've bought Dr. Hallan a couple of new cars in the last year." That was Shane, comparing his goals to Terry's. His remarks were bringing good rounds of laughter from just about everybody. Except Sherri.

She managed to loosen the grip of her fingernails and switched her attention to the little line of neat red grooves they'd left above her elbow. She concentrated for a few moments on steadying her breathing and arranging a more pleasant expression on her face.

She heard the kitchen door bang, then Kyle's voice calling, proving him to be the wonderful brother she'd always thought. "Hey, Sherri! Where do you want these things?"

Sherri wheeled out of the room without a backward glance. The kitchen had never seemed like more of a haven. "Over here." She directed him to set the platter and its huge pile of steaks on the counter. Charcoal-grill odor filled the kitchen, but for once Sherri scarcely noticed it. She started placing the steaks on the serving dish in a meticulously careful arrangement. "Have you met the company yet?"

"No. I haven't left the grill since I went out. Who is it?"

" 'Who are they?' would be more appropriate. It's some friends of the Larsons. We met them once before, but I have a feeling we're going to be seeing a lot more of them real soon."

"Who?"

Sherri stabbed a steak with extra force. "Our prospective stepmother, her parents, and her daughter, from the looks of things."

"What!" He actually shouted it.

"Shh!"

"Stepmother?" Kyle's voice dropped to a near whisper. "What—did Dad say that?"

"Not yet. But you can count on it."

"How do you know?" His words were bordering on an accusation, and his eyes clearly questioned her sanity.

"Go look for yourself. Tell Dad supper will be on in a couple minutes. But then get back here. And bring Tim. I need two people, and at least I know he washed."

He just stood and stared blankly at her.

"Go on." Sherri gave him a little shove. "Hurry up. I don't want these to get cold."

The familiar tasks gave her a much-needed sense of balance. Sherri hurriedly put things together for the table, just in time for Kyle and Tim to take them to the dining room. Kyle had time only to say a quick "I think you're nuts" in her ear before they had to join everyone at the table.

Todd was on her right, Mr. Fallester to her left. Across the table was Shane, between Terry and Kathleen. Sherri felt that her composure was a little better, but she was still glad to close her eyes while her father said the blessing. Dinner was an ordeal. Sherri was determined to keep a low profile, but apparently Mrs. Fallester wasn't going to allow that.

"Goodness, child! I can scarcely believe a girl your age can do a meal like this—everything's so good, and so beautifully put together."

This brought a general murmur of consent from the other guests. Of course, Sherri thought, I don't suppose any of them would disagree aloud. "Thank you." She did her best to smile, but she could feel the stiffness that was still lingering around the edges. "I have a lot of help."

"Help, yes. But, well, how old did you say you were, dear?"

I didn't say—Sherri had to bite back the reply. But she tried to speak carefully. "Fifteen." Really, she thought, maybe I should give up art and try for the stage.

"And you run this house with a pack of men like this around?" Mrs. Fallester seemed sincere enough, but Sherri was squirming under the table-wide attention. Couldn't they think of anything else to talk about? Or did the woman actually think she was being nice?

"Not really. Mrs. Andersen is here most days and does a lot of the meals." Sherri noticed Shane watching her closely from across the table. Hoping he wasn't getting ready to make one of his blunt comments, Sherri was truly surprised when he spoke.

"Yeah, well," he began with his typical, careless ease, "do-it-yourself is the motto out here. Why don't you guys let me take you to the Historical Museum tomorrow afternoon? We could go after school, and it'll give you a chance to see why ranchers are as independent as everybody always accuses us of being."

"But we're supposed to go back tomorrow!" Mr. Fallester protested. "Kathleen's next term starts on Monday, and our flight leaves at two o'clock."

"I doubt it," Terry spoke up in support of his brother. "There's a whopper of a storm that's supposed to come in tonight. It's not likely that any flights will go out for a day or two."

"You're kidding." The old gentleman's statement was almost a plea. "Paul?"

Sherri's father took a quick swallow of coffee. "I'm afraid the boys are probably right. You may be stuck with us for a while."

"I feel like I've been hijacked to Siberia," Mr. Fallester grumbled. He pointed a fork at Shane. "If the weather's going to be so bad, how do you propose to take us anywhere— or even be in school yourself?"

"We'll be fine." Shane grinned. "Four-wheel drive and chains. School will be open tomorrow, and so will the museum. Everybody's used to it."

As the conversation turned to a hot debate between the merits of Wisconsin winters versus Montana winters, Sherri scarcely dared to twitch a finger for fear of recalling attention to herself. The rest of the dinner hour seemed an eternity. Fortunately, the conversation stayed fairly general, and she was able to escape to the kitchen to clean up. But by the time the guests left a couple of hours later, the knots in her stomach hadn't untwisted a bit.

She barely had time to get Tim and Todd into bed and finish her geometry assignment before she had to tumble into bed also. Still, her thoughts were awhirl and sleep was long in coming.

The distraction carried over throughout the next day at school. She paid scant attention in most of her morning classes. *Will he really do it? Will he? Or are you crazy as a loon?* Her mind refused to be still. Lunch hour was a welcome relief. Sherri took her sack lunch to her usual table at the back of the cafeteria, where she propped her literature book open in a vain attempt to read. She should have finished the assignment last night, really. But even now, she couldn't concentrate any better than she'd been able to in class.

All around her, the buzz of activity went on as students ate, chattered, and laughed. Sherri tuned it out with the ease of long practice. Vaguely, she remembered a time when she'd been as much a part of the hubbub as anyone. Swarms of friends used to visit the ranch for such things as birthday parties when she'd been small. And there were the scores of activities that her mother had kept her involved in. But the memories were distant—and a good deal more faded than the actual memories of her mother. Sherri remembered her mom in small, vivid snatches. Breezy cheerfulness. Impressions of a quiet, well-ordered home where nothing was ever late. Hours and hours spent at the kitchen table with paper and crayons.

But the reality was gone, as were the patterns of her early days in elementary school. Most of the changes had been so gradual that Sherri wasn't sure exactly how or when they'd come about. By now, in her sophomore year of high school, the changes had become a barrier between Sherri and most of her classmates. Usually she just tried to ignore it. Her responsibilities with her family demanded a lot of time, and at the end of a school day she was glad enough to heave a sigh of relief and go home. But at times like this, when she sat and watched other girls from her church chatting away at crowded tables, she often had to squash the lid down on a little voice inside that seemed to want to speak up.

She usually found something else to occupy her mind before it could make itself understood. But today there was no trick to keeping her thoughts off her schoolmates. Nothing could compete with the mental turmoil that was not yet twenty-four hours old. Absently Sherri began crumpling up her sandwich bag; then she heard someone speaking to her.

"Hey! Come out of it."

She looked up to see Karen Jennings sitting down opposite her. Karen was one of the few girls that she still kept company with. Like Sherri, Karen was from one of the remoter regions of the county—a ranch south of town, nearly two hours driving time from Rockview. Consequently, they never saw each other during summer vacation, except at an occasional auction or competition. During the school months, Karen was a comfortable companion.

"Hi. Sorry. I was thinking."

"Guess so. What's up? You've been in the clouds all morning."

Sherri shrugged. "I'm tired, I guess. We had company last night. I was up late and didn't get much done."

"Company?" Being from a ranch herself, Karen knew how unusual that was for mid-January when the weather was bad—especially late-night company.

"Yeah. Some friends of the Larsons. They're from Wisconsin."

"Wisconsin?" Karen frowned. "Wisconsin?"

"Yeah. Remember that little state by the lakes with all the trees and no mountains?"

"Hmm. What are they doing out here this time of year?"

Sherri shrugged, thinking better of having brought it up and trying to dismiss the subject. "They're moving. Hey, are we supposed to have a quiz over this stuff today?" She gestured at the book opened before her.

"I don't think so." Karen bit into a sandwich. "Tomorrow, yes."

"Good." Sherri pushed the book aside. "I read it, but I doubt much of it stuck."

Karen paused in her chewing and regarded Sherri with a level look. "By the way, speaking of deadlines, are you going to be in the spring concert this year?"

"No." Sherri finished her demolition of the sandwich bag and threw it into a nearby trash can.

"Why not? This is your second year in choir, and you weren't in last year's concert either. They need more people— or weren't you listening to the announcements this morning?"

"I'm not going to be in it because I can't." Sherri flared briefly. "It means rehearsals two or three nights a week later in the spring. There's no way I can be here, that's all."

Karen sighed. "Well, I know, I guess. But why don't you ever say so? You just act like you couldn't care less. Indifference on two feet."

Sherri stifled a sigh and shrugged.

"Why do you think Miss Kessing gives you such crummy participation scores?"

"As if that was any of your business! What difference does it make to anyone anyway?" Sherri denied the importance of the conversation with vehemence.

The spring concert was one of the biggest projects of the school year, usually involving a small dramatic production, presentations from the band and choir, special comedy, and a lot of smaller variety performances. Sherri heaved another inward sigh, almost wishing that she attended a school that was sports crazy or something-else crazy. But no, she happened to attend one with a heavy ratio of faculty who loved the performing arts. Brighton High School had a reputation for its dramatic productions and music programs. Much of the school's social activity revolved around the auditorium. Either you Were Involved or you Weren't Involved. If you belonged to the latter group, Sherri guessed, you were supposed to become a hermit and do penance for the rest of your life.

The paper bag was gone, so Sherri fiddled with the handle on her purse. The dramatic, artistic spirit of the productions did appeal to her immensely. But how could she afford to admit it? Even now she usually felt like an apple living among oranges. She pushed aside thoughts of the concert and took a firmer grasp on her knowledge that she was needed at home. The conversation with Karen didn't improve, and Sherri went to her next class with her friend's comments still rankling in her mind.

What does she know about *indifference?* Sherri wondered with a tinge of venom. I could fall down dead in the hallway, and all these people would just step over me and go about their business.

As soon as Sherri stepped off the school bus, she felt the weight lift from her shoulders the way it always did. She changed clothes and spent some time in the small indoor ring drilling Tramp, one of the young horses that her father wanted to sell in the spring. But even while she was riding him, and throughout the rest of her routine duties—finishing up the supper preparations that Mrs. Andersen had already started and setting the table, she couldn't keep from speculating on when and how she was going to hear more about Lynn Merriell. As it turned out, she didn't have much longer to wonder.

When supper was over, her dad brought out the family Bible for their evening reading. Usually he just read a chapter or two and then asked a couple of them to pray before he closed. Tonight he was reading from Isaiah chapter thirty. Normally, Isaiah was one of Sherri's favorite books. She loved to hear the proclamations of the ancient prophet about God's guidance and protection of His people and the things that were foretold for the nation of Israel.

"*And though the Lord give you the bread of adversity, and the water of affliction, yet shall not thy teachers be removed into a corner any more, but thine eyes shall see thy teachers,*" her father read in his usual, steady voice. "*And thine ears shall hear a word behind thee, saying, This is the way, walk ye in it, when ye turn to the right hand, and when ye turn to the left.*"

Sherri wasn't even surprised when her father closed the Bible and said, "Tonight I want to tell you about a special application of those verses—an application that has already affected my life, and one that's going to affect each one of you."

Sherri looked up from her plate. Without moving her head, she ran her eyes around the table. All five of her brothers listened with their usual attention. A faint curiosity, perhaps, but nothing to indicate that any of them realized what was about to be said.

"Before your mother and I were married, we made an agreement that if either of us were taken while there were still children in our home, we would ask the Lord to provide another partner for us. At the time we made the agreement, it seemed like a superfluous thing." He stopped to clear his throat. Sherri thought he looked nervous.

"Of course, it's been years since your mother went to be with the Lord." Another long pause. "But it's taken a while for me to find the lady I thought should be that one. I've had the Lord's leading in this, just as clearly as those verses say—that the Lord will direct us in which way to walk and which way to turn."

Sherri realized that Kyle, directly across the table, was staring at her. She permitted herself the luxury of one tiny smile. Unbelievably slow, she thought. But her father was still talking.

"Kids, there doesn't seem to be any gradual way for me to say this, except just to blurt out that I'm going to be getting married again. I hadn't intended that it was going to turn out to be a surprise. I wanted you to be able to take a while to get to know her, but there just didn't seem to be any way with her so far away. I'm sure, by now, that none of you has any doubt that the woman is Lynn Merriell."

Her father paused, rubbing the back of his hand across his eyes. "And, too, I guess it was just hard to talk about, for me. I'd decided I wanted to tell you all at once sometime this month. Then this unexpected trip came up for them and, presto, here they were. Even though it was impromptu, I felt that it was high time you all met them. I've grown to love Lynn very much, and I believe it would be best for everyone if she and Kathleen were a part of our family here."

Sherri, having already spent a lot of time digesting this expected announcement, was at this point far more interested in her brothers' reactions. Terry and Shane both seemed delighted, judging by their grins. Kyle was still staring at

Sherri in a vaguely stupefied fashion. Todd was frowning, and Timmy looked puzzled.

"You mean she's going to live here?" Tim clearly wasn't sure of the implications.

"Um-hmm." He turned to his youngest son with a smile. "She's going to be your new mom."

"Really?" That did it. A huge smile broke over the little boy's face.

Sherri was suprised at the surge of jealousy that shot through her. Well, she's not going to be my "mom," she thought, feeling an unexpected longing for the blonde woman who was so distant in her childhood memories.

A long discussion ensued. The wedding had been set for the last weekend in April, just a few weeks before the end of the school year. Lynn would be in Wisconsin between now and then, although their father would be making a trip there in March. The ceremony itself would be here in Montana.

After that. . . . Well, there goes the neighborhood, Sherri thought dismally. I can't believe this is happening. She felt the weight of reality settle heavily over her. She took up staring at her plate again until the last detail had been hashed out by the rest of the family and she could escape to her room.

Not for several days did Sherri have much to say about the prospect of the wedding. She particularly avoided the issue around her father, until Saturday night. As usual, she was in the laundry room pressing shirts for Tim and Todd. She'd gone on permanent strike a year or so before as far as the older guys were concerned. Either they put their ironing out in time for Mrs. Andersen to do, they ironed their own, or they wore wrinkles. But Todd and Tim still required last-minute pinch-hitting, lest they appear in church looking as if they'd slept in—or on—their clothes.

"Sherri?" Tim's discouraged voice barely reached her from where he sat at the kitchen table.

"Hmm?"

"I can't learn this. It's too long." A dramatic sigh followed the statement, and Sherri heard a pair of feet hit the floor. Steps followed, and a small, dark head peeked around the doorway. "Can't I go downstairs and help Kyle finish fixing his saddle?"

"No, love. You can't." Sherri shook her head at him with a sigh of her own. "You know you should have learned the verses earlier. Now you're stuck till you can say them to me."

"They're too long!" Tim's voice rose a fraction.

"They're no longer than last week's. Quit reading them and start saying them. In fact—" Sherri set the iron down and grabbed him by the waist, hoisting him onto the dryer. "Sit there and tell me what you can remember of the verses. Start talking."

Tim rolled his eyes and banged his heels on the front of the dryer, but he started in hesitantly. "Proverbs 3:5-7. Trust in the Lord with all thine heart; and lean not unto thine own understanding. In . . . " his voice trailed away.

"All." Sherri prompted.

"In all. In all thy ways acknowledge him, and . . . and . . . and he shall direct . . . um . . . thy paths. Be . . . "

"Be not wise."

"Be not wise."

"Go on." Sherri waited. Tim was silent. "Start over," she said.

"Sherri!" He was almost wailing.

"Tim, it's your own fault. You've had all week to work on them."

"I don't want to learn any more dumb verses!" This time he shouted and swung both feet against the dryer with all his strength. The resulting boom would have shamed a regiment of kettledrums. Before Sherri even had time to react, their father was in the doorway to the laundry room. Tim froze.

Without a word, her father took the two steps separating him from his youngest son and plucked him off the dryer.

Setting Tim down facing the door, his dad marched him through the kitchen, propelling him by a hand on the back of the neck. They disappeared into the hall on the other side, headed for the ranch office.

Sherri returned to her ironing, feeling disheartened. What a way for a kid to end a Saturday, she thought. You have to get with it earlier in the week, she rebuked herself. Make sure they get their memory verses learned. This is as much your fault as his.

She'd hung up the shirts and was in the kitchen getting herself a cup of cocoa when her father reappeared. "Want some?" She gestured with the cup she'd just taken a swallow from.

"No." He sat down heavily on the old sofa in the corner. "Sherri, why is it Saturday night and Tim still doesn't know his Sunday school lesson?"

Sherri started to make a quick response, then traded it for a long swallow of cocoa. "I goofed," she said simply. "I let him put it off."

Her father passed a hand over his eyes and heaved a sigh. "Well, I can't blame you, really." A long moment of silence followed. Sherri listened to the clock tick. "It's with this kind of thing that I hope to see a lot of pressure relieved for all of us, Sherri."

Her heart made a quick jump for her throat, then subsided.

"We're doing all right," he continued. "But God has an ideal plan for families, and I'm thankful that He's provided a way for us to have that ideal again."

Ideal! Sherri's thoughts screamed. She studied the remaining cocoa in the bottom of her cup for a moment. She was surprised to hear herself speak aloud. "I think we're just fine the way we are." She hadn't intended to say it, but the words were out—and all the much more forceful for their quietness.

Her father slowly lowered the hand that was still in front of his eyes. He stared at his daughter. Sherri drained her cup and turned away to rinse it. She waited for a rebuke and was surprised at his words.

"So . . . do you know your verses for tomorrow?"

"Yes, sir."

"Let's hear them."

Sherri shook the water from the cup and set it down before she started. *"And it came to pass, when Moses had made an end of writing the words of this law in a book, until they were finished, That Moses commanded the Levites, which bare the ark of the covenant of the Lord, saying, Take this book of the law, and put it in the side of the ark of the covenant of the Lord your God, that it may be there for a witness against thee.* Deuteronomy 31:24-26." She took a breath and plunged into the second part. *"God, who at sundry times and in divers manners spake in time past unto the fathers by the prophets, Hath in these last days spoken unto us by his Son, whom he hath appointed heir of all things, by whom also he made the worlds.* Hebrews 1:1-2."

Her dad looked thoughtful. "What are you studying?"

"We just started a new section. It's about the inspiration and preservation of God's Word. We're going to be talking about different translations and things, too, I guess. And some of the history of the English Bible."

"That ought to be interesting."

"Um-hmm. I like Mr. Riley. He starts studies on things that we're interested in, and he doesn't get miffed if you ask him a question."

Her father chuckled. "Ask all the questions you want, Sherri. That's what a study like that's for." He started to get up. Sherri took a breath. It was a rare chance these days to catch him alone.

"Dad?"

"Hmm?" He stretched and went to peer out the window into the darkness.

"Do you think I'm ever really going to be able to take those drawing lessons?"

"It'll be forty below zero by morning," he commented. Sherri wondered if he'd even heard, until he turned back to face her. "I don't see why not. It's going to have to wait until we can get on top of the schedule around here a little, though. How about we look into something this summer when school's out?" He tested the latch on the door. "But we've got to get to bed if we're ever going to get up tomorrow, okay?"

Sherri nodded, straining against the tears that were forming. She did a frantic search of her mind for something else to say. He's not deliberately putting me off. I know that. He just doesn't understand. *Well, say something then.* Ask him if you can bring some of Mom's pictures downstairs to practice from. That ought to get his attention.

But no words would come to bridge the awkwardness of the moment. Or maybe she was the only one who felt awkward. He just yawned and started toward the hall. "Get the lights, will you, Sherri?"

"Sure. Good night, Dad."

"Night, honey. See you tomorrow."

Only the beginnings of a cramp in her arm made Sherri realize she was gripping the edge of the sink with all her strength. She relaxed her hold and folded her arms. "Lord, why do I never get anywhere with this?" She was scarcely aware that she spoke aloud. "Is the desire something You gave to me, or do I just want to do it for *me?* I think I need an answer."

Chapter Three

The loud jangling of the alarm clock jerked Sherri rudely from her comfortable world of slumber. The cold bit at her hands and face as she reached to turn off the clock. Sherri hurriedly retreated under the blankets and pulled them over her head. Winter mornings in the ranch house were bitter cold. A glass of water sitting on the window ledge would freeze during the night. It took another five minutes before Sherri could summon the courage to leap from bed, grab her robe, and dash for the shower.

She barely made it this morning. She always set her alarm for a few minutes before the guys' alarms went off at five. That gave her first grabs at the bathroom. But this particular morning, her few moments of delay meant that she was barely there before someone was rapping at the door.

"Hurry up, Sherri!"

Mornings in the James home moved on split-second timing. Many things had to be done, and the one and only school bus made its appearance at seven. Sherri was exempt from morning corral duties during the school months. She had breakfast to make, clean-up to take care of, lunches to pack, and Tim and Todd to supervise—not to mention getting herself ready. Mrs. Andersen didn't come to the ranch until nine o'clock.

EVERY PERFECT GIFT

This morning, Sherri had the sausage on the grill and was cracking eggs before she remembered that it was her birthday. Sixteen, she thought in amazement. It didn't seem very long ago that she'd felt that sixteen was basically adult. Sherri made a face at the eggs. She sure didn't feel adult. Especially not during these last few weeks.

Life around the ranch had seemed to go on as normal since that Week of the Announcement. No one but Tim and Todd talked much about it anymore. Sherri tried to play along with the game and pretend that the issue wasn't consuming her, body and soul. At least five times a day, she resisted the urge to knock her brothers' heads together. She wanted to shout at them—How can you be so complacent? Don't you realize what's going to happen?

But the guys, apparently having thought it out and concluded that most of the changes affecting them would be positive, seemed to summarily dismiss everything in a way that drove Sherri wild. A dozen thoughts a day fell over each other for first consideration in her mind. She wondered who would get the bathroom first in the mornings now? Did this mean 4:30 A.M. for her? What was she going to talk to this woman about, anyway? Sherri hadn't had the impression that Lynn was going to be riding herd with them.

Was the woman going to be a take-charge tyrant—furious if crossed by a quarter of an inch? Or would she be just a silent addition that did nothing but make others feel uncomfortable—as though they were constantly living with formal guests in the house?

"Happy birthday!"

Her father's voice interrupted her thoughts that were, as usual, scrambling faster than the eggs.

"Morning, Dad. Thanks." Sherri turned from the stove and began pulling dishes from the cupboard.

"You don't look any older," he commented as he went to the sink to wash. "Still my little girl. I don't care if you are sixteen."

No, Sherri thought later. I expect I don't look any older. She pulled on her boots and coat, wrapping a scarf securely around her throat.

"Tim! Come on. Hurry up!" She stood impatiently by the door. She didn't dare walk out before him, or he'd wind up missing the bus. Shane had already departed for the bus stop with Todd.

Finally, she was following her little brother up the driveway. The morning darkness was thinner than usual. The days of late February were lengthening once again, hinting at an approaching springtime.

What does make a person look older, Sherri wondered. On the bus, she took a seat as close to the heater as she could manage. It seemed that so many of her classmates had shot toward maturity in the last couple of years. It wasn't their looks or their size. It was more of something in the way they talked and the things they talked about. Something of a new confidence in the way they acted.

Just the other day, she'd heard Janelle and Katie talking about various college programs. As she'd tuned in her radar to the conversation, she realized that they'd both already applied and been accepted at the university of their choice. That had rocked Sherri's mind for the rest of the day. College! Yes, she knew she wanted to go. How else could she ever get a chance to get anywhere in the art field? But it seemed so far away—far in the future, and at least a million miles from Rockview . . . and anyway, the thought of approaching her father about what she wanted to do—well! Would he even take her seriously?

But in almost the same thought came the realization— faster than she wanted it—that elementary school didn't seem so far away, either, and that was a lot farther back than two years. Well, I *am* sixteen, Sherri told herself with a note of finality as she stepped off the bus at school. Surely that will make some sort of difference.

Maybe, or maybe not.

Obviously not, Sherri had decided by the time she joined the lunch line. How is it, she wondered, that I can go through a whole day without so much as speaking to another person? Do I just look like part of the scenery, or what? On days like today when Karen is gone, no one even notices that I'm here.

Even the kids from her church rarely paid much attention to Sherri. They always seemed to be completely involved in events and interests about which Sherri knew nothing. I wonder what they'd say if I just went over and plopped my tray down at their table, Sherri thought, watching the animated conversation at a table where she knew several girls. She considered it for about two seconds, but she couldn't summon the courage. She remembered the last time she'd tried something like that. The entire conversation had been about some tobogganing party that they were all going to that weekend. Obviously, it was nothing to which she'd been invited, and no one had seemed to pay the slightest attention to the fact that she was sitting there. Sherri hadn't even been sure what all they were saying, so she couldn't contribute anything. She had wound up just sitting there, feeling stupid and out of place, the humiliation of being such an obvious outsider biting deeper by the second.

That's what it's always like, Sherri grumbled inwardly as she put her tray down on her customary table by the far wall. All the advice tells you to "strike up small talk. Go out of your way to be friendly. Speak first, etc." But what does it matter if they haven't an ounce of interest in anything that you could say? They couldn't care less that I'm glad Todd didn't catch Timmy's flu, or that the bay colt is going to be the best cow horse we've trained in a long time, or that we're already gearing up for spring work at home. Sherri was unnecessarily rough in tearing open her carton of milk.

Ye shall be witnesses unto me. The little voice caught her by surprise this time. She didn't have time to tune it out.

"I know, Lord." Sherri responded silently. "But a lot of them don't even know who I am. I can't just walk up to them out of the blue and say 'By the way, there's something I want you to know.' " Not only wouldn't they listen, but the next time they saw me, they'd run. She wrestled her thoughts back to her tuna sandwich and wound up rewrapping the rest of it, having somehow lost her appetite. In a left-field attempt to occupy her mind, she reread her literature assignment for the next class period.

Sherri climbed on the bus that afternoon feeling strangely dejected. Katie Forrester settled in the seat in front of her and turned halfway around. "Sherri, do you have the page numbers for the geometry assignment?" Katie frowned as she spoke. "I can't find the paper where I wrote them down."

"Sure." Sherri fumbled through her books until she found her own scribblings. "It's pages 231-235, all the even-numbered proofs."

"Oh, yuk!" Katie complained as she wrote the page numbers in her notebook. "I'm never going to get all that done tonight. I have rehearsal at seven—I have a solo in the spring concert this year. Did I tell you that yet?"

You haven't told me anything in six months, Sherri said silently. Aloud she said, "Oh, really?"

"Yes! I'm so excited!" Katie went on. "This theme on the American West this year is just the best idea since, well, since I don't know what."

She always has been kind of a jabbermouth, Sherri thought as she half-listened. Katie had visited church a couple of times with Janelle but wasn't, to the best of her knowledge, a Christian.

"Why don't you ever get into the concerts?" Katie was silent long enough for Sherri to need to think of an answer.

"It's kind of hard to keep up with the time schedule. I live a long ways out. Plus things have been really busy at home in the last year or so. Dad bought out another rancher to the east of us and—"

"Oh, yeah?" Katie answered, her eyes already shifting across the aisle. "Hey Randy! Can I get a ride home with you tonight? Mom's going to drop me off, but I need a ride home."

Sherri fell silent and began twisting the spiral on her notebook. "Dear Lord, what do I always say that's wrong?" She had the spiral worked almost all the way out of the papers before Kyle dropped into the seat beside her. He was barely in time, for the bus started chugging away.

"So, how's the birthday?" he asked. His eyes were searching her face rather thoroughly.

"How could any day in school be much different from another?" Sherri heard the tinge of bitterness in her own voice. Kyle had the good sense not to answer.

The bus was well out of town before Sherri spoke again. "Kyle, do you ever have a hard time talking to the kids who live in town?"

"Hard time—what do you mean?"

"Well, just as if there weren't a lot of things that you had in common."

"Shoot, no." Kyle slid down in his seat and propped his knees up on the back of the seat before him. "Most of the guys love to hear about ranch stuff. I think most of the kids here would love to live where we do."

"Easy for you to say," Sherri retorted. But she knew that he spoke the truth. It was different for guys, she thought. Kyle, and Terry and Shane before him, always had an eager following of friends any time they wanted company at the ranch. Nor did any of them ever seem to lack company at school, Sherri realized. So what's the matter with me? She thought about the "horse-crazy" girls who were always fighting over the new stories in the library. Sherri had always pretty much taken the horses for granted. They were there; they were fun, and you had to be able to ride well to enjoy them. Of course, she especially loved her own two. But horses weren't anything to dream about, in her opinion. Sherri's thoughts inched back several weeks to the woman doing the sketches at the mall.

As usual, the dejection lasted no longer than it took for her to step off the bus. The icy wind cut into her, driving particles of snow through the heavy scarf. Beautiful Rockview! Sherri inhaled sharply, making her lungs ache with the cold. The ranch buildings were nestled into the snowdrifts, standing out in contrast to the towering mountains behind them—mountains with dark, evergreen forests and endless miles of white, frozen slopes.

Sherri took off at a run through the drifts of snow. Slinging her book bag and purse over her shoulder, she stretched out her arms to embrace the knifing air. "I'll beat you there!" Kyle pushed past Shane and came by her at a run.

"Like fun you will!" Sherri spurted ahead and drew near enough to shove him sprawling into the new, loose snow.

A threatening shout from Shane, farther behind, put wings on her feet. Sherri sped away from them, plunging through drifts and taking uneven, sliding steps to keep her balance. Spurred on by the certainty of a freezing face wash, she beat them to the kitchen door by a hair—but this time a miss was as good as a mile. For as soon as Sherri was inside on this particular night, she reigned as queen.

Dinner was fun. Her dad put the guys to work in the kitchen, refusing to let Sherri touch a single spoon or pot, either for preparation or for cleanup. They moaned and groaned, but did a nice job anyway. Sherri looked at the mounds of fresh trout to be grilled outside, knowing that her father must have made a special trip to town today because he knew what she liked more than anything else. And with it, baked potatoes, sour cream, fruit salad, and broccoli-cheese casserole. Sherri's mouth was watering already as she thought of the flaky trout. Charcoal smell filled the air.

"What weird tastes." Terry kept up a mock complaint throughout the meal. But no one complained when Kyle carried in a triple-layer chocolate cake, to be followed by the unanimous favorite: homemade cookies 'n cream ice cream.

Mrs. Andersen must have been busy today, Sherri thought.

When the cake had been served, Sherri could finally begin unwrapping the gifts that were sitting in the middle of the table. They made up a varied assortment: cards and small remembrances from out-of-state relatives; a sweater from Terry; a new pair of loafers from Todd and Tim—through her father, Sherri knew—and a beautiful, handwoven saddle blanket of red, blue, and tan wool. Sherri looked up at her father when she realized what it was.

"You bought this way last fall!" she exclaimed in amazement. "At the Apache Craft Fair!"

"How could I not have?" Her father smiled at her. "After the fuss you made over it."

"Oh, thank you, Dad! It's lovely! And it's just perfect for Taffy's coloring."

The last package on the table was strangely lumpy and carried Shane's name on the tag. She shot him a look of curiosity, but he was carefully concealing any expression.

She removed the paper and stared entranced at what fell out into her lap: a bundle of professional artist's pencils, a thick sketch pad of heavy paper, and a heavy, softbound book, titled *Illustrating for the Advanced Amateur*. For several moments, Sherri didn't even think to thank her brother. Her attention was riveted on the pencils—there were different weights, varying degrees of softness, and several shadings of basic colors. Then she opened the book and saw the beautiful step-by-step sketches with their detailed explanations. Not until she came across what had been written in the front of the book did she look up.

"To Sherri," it said, "on her sixteenth birthday, with hopes that it will help her toward her goals."

"Thank you, Shane." Sherri looked up and spoke quietly, but she thought Shane probably knew the weight her words carried. He was still looking at her with an intent, unreadable expression.

Quickly, she ducked her head back into the book. How did he know? she wondered. I haven't said all that much. Of course, he knows that I fool around with sketches, but I've never said anything about "goals."

Sherri was still wondering about it when she climbed into bed. Could it be that her doubts and wishes weren't as well concealed as she thought? Well, she answered herself, there's not much you can do about it unless Dad ever really does come through with the drawing lessons, and that—she made a face at the ceiling to emphasize her thought—that would take a *miracle*. She let out her breath in a sigh as she reached over and clicked off the lamp.

Chapter Four

Sunshine streamed through the open window of the second-floor geometry classroom. Inside, Sherri sat at her desk, fidgeting with her pencil. This bright spring day had seemed to drag on into a period that was about ten years long. Yet at the same time she wished it would never end. When she arrived home from school today, Lynn Merriell would be there. Lynn James now, she corrected herself.

Nearly four months had passed since the evening that Sherri's father had told them he was going to remarry. Sherri's thoughts drifted back over the wedding that had taken place two weeks ago. For the most part it was a merciful blur in her mind. She hadn't enjoyed the ceremony or the attention that scores of people had lavished on the family. Much less had she enjoyed fielding the comments. How did she like the idea of the change in the family? Wasn't it going to make things a lot easier for her? She must be excited about having another woman at the ranch, etc., etc.

What do they expect me to say? Sherri thought, stifling a growing urge to do something violent. Am I supposed to lie? I'd catch it for sure if I told them the truth. Somehow she'd perfected the art of mumbling a half-answer—something that was enough to qualify as an answer, but noncommittal enough to keep her conscience clear.

EVERY PERFECT GIFT

As the day of the wedding approached, Sherri had grown accustomed to having tension headaches nearly every day. Nervous energy piled up inside, most of which she tried to expend in a wild flurry of activity. Closets and corners that had been given licks-and-promises for months on end were torn apart, sorted, and scrubbed. Sherri was determined that every square inch of the house would be in first-class shape.

She'd finally worked up the nerve to tell Karen. Her friend seemed pleased in a way but was openly skeptical of Lynn's future on a ranch.

"Does she ride or anything?"

"I don't know. She says so. But you know how that goes."

"Yeah." Karen frowned. "Well, look on the bright side," she'd said philosophically. "It should give you a lot more free time."

"That's what everybody keeps telling me, but at what price? She drives me nuts already, and I hardly know her. She just . . . well, she goes everywhere looking like she just stepped out of a magazine. I have a feeling we're going to hate each other. I don't know what good she can possibly be to the ranch, and I'll never be like her."

Karen cocked an eyebrow at her. "It might be good for you."

"So I've been told." Sherri couldn't let her friend see how deeply that remark bit. "A double dose, no less. Kathleen, too."

"Well, don't forget: they're the newcomers, not you. You're already a part of the ranch. They can't take that away from you, so loosen up a little."

By the wedding ceremony, Sherri felt that if she were any looser she would come unglued. She sat beside Tim and Todd, feeling very out of place. She'd spent several long sessions behind the locked door in her room, trying to figure out what to wear that day. Her father had been so absorbed in his own thoughts that Sherri hadn't been able to work up the nerve to approach him about the possibility of getting something new.

After hours of trial and error, she finally settled on a silky-feeling rose dress that someone had given to her the year before but she'd never worn. Shane had caught her sneaking through the hall to inspect it in the bathroom mirror.

"Well, well, well." His tone was typically teasing. But something else told Sherri that he was at least partially serious. "Looks like having Lynn and Kathleen around is going to force some civilization on you."

Sherri had been glad for the dim light in the hall. It concealed the flush of embarrassment on her face. But then Shane had really surprised her.

"It looks nice, Sherri. Really. It's a good color on you." He paused, and the teasing tone came back. "I remember when Aunt Lindy gave it to you last Christmas. What have you been doing with it? Using it for a saddle pad?"

Sherri shrugged and brushed past him into the bathroom. Half of surviving brothers was knowing when to ignore them. But no matter how much she fussed, she still couldn't seem to cope with her hair. Sherri had wound up having some of its thick length cut off before the wedding. At least it stayed in a semblance of order when it was shorter.

With a start, Sherri jerked back to reality. The teacher's eye was on her, and she turned her attention to the formula she was supposed to be working out. Her attention didn't stay on geometry very long, though. How could it? Today was zero hour. Her father had called this morning while they were at the breakfast table. He'd spoken to Terry. They would be home around noon.

Sherri tightened her grip on the pencil. She'd been dreading this day, but she wasn't sure she could have stated her reasons. Lynn hadn't ever been anything but nice to her during the times they'd talked—well, not that they really talked. Lynn talked, and Sherri mumbled an occasional reply. She could never think of much to say.

I hope she'll just leave me alone, Sherri thought.

Fortunately, or unfortunately, depending on how she was thinking at the moment, this was the last class period of the day. There was nothing else between her and the return to the ranch.

Sherri stared at the numbers on the paper before her until they swam into a blur. She wondered how soon Kathleen would be back from college—she'd taken time off from classes to attend the wedding, of course. She'd been her mother's maid of honor. Immediately afterward Kathleen had returned to the college she attended, but the relief would be temporary. Sherri figured it wouldn't be more than a couple of weeks. Regular school was going to be out in less than a month, and normally, colleges let out before then. Sherri closed her eyes and heaved a sigh. If there was anything she dreaded more than Lynn, it was Lynn and Kathleen together.

She gave up the struggle for concentration and started drawing sketches of horses in the margin of her notebook. At least she looked like she was doing something—she hoped.

When the bell finally sounded, Sherri froze in her place. All her impatience seemed to vanish through the open door as the other students began to leave. Suddenly she slammed her book shut, pulled her things together, and jumped up into the aisle—running squarely into another girl coming from the back of the room.

"Hey, Sherri! Watch it!" The girl looked at her with disgust.

"Sorry, Carla." Sherri ducked her head and hurried out of the room. She made a quick stop at her locker, then hurried out to the bus. Dodging into a front seat, she dropped her books beside her, hoping to save the seat for Kyle.

Tim and Todd scrambled aboard together. "Hi, Sherri!" Their voices chimed in unison.

"Hi, guys."

They took the seat behind her and proceeded to hang over the back of hers. "Aren't you excited, Sherri? Do you think she's gonna be mean? Or fun? At least you won't be the only girl around, now."

Sherri didn't answer. They weren't expecting her to, really. At least if they were, they weren't giving her any time to answer. So she settled herself back in the seat and shrugged.

Kyle showed up barely ahead of the main swarm. Sherri scraped up her books, and he collapsed beside her. "Whew!" He sounded like she felt. "I thought that day would never get done with. Lucky for Shane. I wish I was a senior."

"It was long, all right." Sherri kept her voice low. "Except I don't know why. I'm not any happier to be going home." She chose to ignore his comment about Shane. All seniors were being dismissed early these last few days of school. Shane's refusal to let them forget it was grinding enough without discussing it.

"Why don't you want to go home?" Kyle looked puzzled. "That's all I've wanted to do all day!"

"Yeah, well, not me."

"Are you off your nut? We've all been sitting around wondering about this woman for ages."

"I'm just not sure if I'm going to like what I find out."

"Well, better to know than to wonder."

"Not always," Sherri countered. "I can think of a lot of bad things that I wish I didn't know."

Kyle rolled his eyes and kept quiet.

When the bus pulled to a stop at Rockview, Tim and Todd were out the door like a shot. Like a twin-drive machine, they tore off up the driveway. Sherri had a feeling Kyle would have followed them if she hadn't been dragging her feet so much in getting off the bus.

"Come on!" he exclaimed, half-turning to watch her step off.

Sherri frowned. She looked toward the house. Sure enough. There was Lynn's car parked in front of the patio.

"Sherri!" There was growing impatience in Kyle's voice. He was eager to be at the house, but she could tell he didn't want to leave her. He knew she was uncomfortable—though he didn't really understand why.

"You go ahead. I'm coming."

"You are not."

"Please? Kyle, please go." Sherri just stood, biting her lip.

"Oh, forget it." He turned and hurried away. Not running, actually. But walking fast.

Sherri started after him, mainly because she felt conspicuous standing at the end of the driveway. She meandered along, hugging her geometry book. She kept her eyes away from the house, scanning the budding green in the mountain slopes above. When she came to the sidewalk that led to the patio, her feet just carried her right on by. Without really thinking about it, she went around to the door at the far end of the house—the one that came in at the end of the hall by her bedroom.

Quietly Sherri slipped into her room. Even from the other end of the house she could hear the laughing and talking. It sounded like everyone in the world was in the den, though she couldn't really make out anything specific that was being said.

Sherri knew that she was just calling attention to herself by being absent. That was the last thing she wanted, but somehow—she stopped as she caught her reflection in the mirror. She faced it with a long stare, setting her books down and dropping into the chair before the table.

With a sigh, she propped her chin on her hands. Her face was already tanned from being in the spring sun so much. Her hair was hanging around her shoulders in a cascade of unruly curls. Frizzy, she thought dismally, sweeping her reflection in a quick survey that ran from the hair to the blue shirt and straight plaid skirt to Terry's varsity jacket and then to the scuffed loafers. She scrutinized her short, stubby fingers that were still ink-stained from the afternoon's art class.

A burst of soprano laughter from the den made her remember Lynn's polished appearance. "This is ridiculous!" She whispered the rebuke to herself, but she didn't get up.

Shane's comments still festered. *Maybe this is going to force some civilization on you.*

Sherri sighed and looked away from the mirror. She went back to biting her lip until she heard footsteps in the hallway.

"Sherri?" Her father's voice reached her.

She didn't answer, but he kept coming. Someone must have seen her come in.

"Sherri?" He reached the bedroom door. "Hey, girl—what are you doing? I haven't even had a hug yet!"

"Hi, Daddy!" Sherri jumped up and flung herself into his arms, ignoring the questioning look in his eyes.

"Well, now that's more like it," he said as he held her in a bear hug.

Sherri wasn't sure where the tears came from, but she felt two huge ones welling out. There was no hiding them when he released her.

"Oh, boy." His voice was teasing. "Either you're really glad to see me or else your brothers have driven you crazy while I was gone."

"Some of both, I guess," she said, forcing a smile. She was glad for any explanation.

"Come on—you have to get in on hearing all the stories." He put an arm around her shoulders and led her down the hall.

Sherri wanted nothing less than to "hear all the stories," but there wasn't any way around it. She followed her dad into the den, acknowledging Lynn's bright greeting without meeting the woman's eyes. Timmy and Todd were seated on either side of her, and she had an arm around each. Sherri turned her eyes away from the little boys' contented expressions.

"All right." Her father took over the conversation. "Sherri, I was in the middle of telling them about the Gettysburg battlefield."

Sherri chose a seat on the ottoman at the very edge of the group. She sat with arms folded and resting on her knees and tried to pay attention to what her dad was saying. It was hard. She could smell Lynn's perfume, and she couldn't look at her father without seeing her stepmother. She felt the woman's presence like a physical, tangible pressure.

From time to time, she sensed rather than saw Lynn's eyes on her. "What in the world is she thinking?" Sherri wondered as she twisted a piece of blonde hair around her finger.

Her father's story finally ended. Sherri lost track of the conversation for a moment, but her attention snapped back when everyone made a dive for a sheaf of pictures that he brought out.

She took advantage of the brief shuffle to do what she'd been craving to do since she'd stepped into the room. She mumbled something about supper and slipped into the hallway. With a huge sigh of relief, she almost ran for the kitchen.

Another surprise awaited her, however. Before she even reached the kitchen door she caught the smell of frying chicken. Rounding the corner and bursting into the room, she saw Mrs. Andersen loading the oven with pan after pan of risen bread dough. Several kettles simmered busily away on the stove.

"Hello, Sherri, hon." Mrs. Andersen straightened up slowly. "What you doin' here?"

"I came to see about supper." Sherri heard her own voice as short and brusque.

"Well, your stepmom was here afore you. She thought your family would be liking an earlier supper tonight. Sort of like a good get-acquainted session."

Sherri felt a frown take over her face. She crossed to the stove and started pulling lids off pans to inspect their contents. Potatoes, fresh corn, swiftly browning chicken.

"Must be gonna take a big load off you, havin' a woman in the right place in this house again." Mrs. Andersen stood there and looked at Sherri. "It's been a long time."

Still no answer from Sherri.

"Might be so that you're not even remembering."

"No, I don't remember, really."

"Well, you was just a mite yerself. You've had to grow up uncommon fast. Though myself, I don't think it hurt ya much."

"What time is supper supposed to be?" asked Sherri quickly.

"Half hour, probably. Fivish, or thereabouts. Myself, I'm headed on home now."

"Bye," Sherri said distractedly. She went to the refrigerator and took out a Coke. Pulling the top off, she wandered out the screen door and across the back patio. Dash, the German shepherd, greeted her enthusiastically.

"Hi, boy." Sherri patted his head. She made her way to a chair in the shade. The dog followed her, sitting down at her feet and leaning against her knees.

"What do you think of this, Dash?" She rubbed the shepherd's ears absently. He groaned in appreciation.

"I just feel so dumb around her. And it makes me mad that she's here at all. Nothing's going to be the same anymore."

Sherri took a long swallow of the Coke. "Plus, everybody seems to think I should be turning inside out with delight about the whole deal. Pardon me if I don't froth at the mouth, but I guess I'm the casual type."

Sherri fell silent for a while as she watched Luke and Dandy, way down at the corrals. The foreman and the grizzled old hand were running a herd of cattle into the north pasture. "Nobody seems to think that it should bother me at all. Or maybe the problem is all with me. I don't know. I just don't know how to act."

Sherri sat in the chair until the commotion in the kitchen told her that everyone else was getting ready for supper. Heaving a sigh, she went back inside and joined the general shuffle that was progressing toward the dining room.

Sherri was aware of her father's eyes on her, but he didn't say anything. That alone relieved her, not to mention that no one so much as commented on her absence. The dinner would probably have been delicious if Sherri could have tasted any of it. As it was, if she hadn't looked in the kitchen earlier, she probably wouldn't have known what she was eating.

Nevertheless, she kept her attention on her plate rather than meeting the eyes of anyone around her. Not until they were halfway through dessert did anyone make a direct attempt to draw her into the conversation. Even then, she didn't realize it right away. When her father's voice finally got through to her, she could tell by his tone that it wasn't the first time he'd spoken.

"What do you think, Sherri?"

"Hmm? I'm sorry. My mind wandered a little."

"So I see. I was wondering how you felt about being able to retire as cook?"

"Oh, yeah. Well." Sherri groped desperately for something to say. "That ought to give me some free time, hmm? I'm not sure I'll know how to act." Not very elegant, she thought wryly, but certainly truthful.

A general laugh ran around the table, sparking a hope in Sherri that maybe she looked like she was carrying this off better than she'd thought. Her father's response was nearly as dry as her own.

"I'm sure we can think of something to keep you busy—but even so, we'll expect no complaining out of you for the next six months, then."

"Doesn't she even have to help?" Timmy's voice was incredulous.

"Of course," Sherri's father replied steadily, with a note of amusement. "Everybody does. Just like always. But Sherri's had to do a lot extra for a long time. Now Lynn is here to take over."

Sherri barely kept from flinching at the last two words. Lynn's quick response—too quick, Sherri thought—said that she'd caught the reaction.

"I'm going to need a lot of help, Sherri." The woman's smile was beautiful. "There's so much I don't know."

Don't patronize me! Sherri bit back the words just before they leaped out. "Sure," she said, returning her attention to her plate.

Sherri was certain that dinner lasted three or four hours. When it finally seemed to be drawing to a close, she found herself on her feet, volunteering Shane and Kyle to help her do the dishes and clean up the kitchen. "That way you guys can relax some." Mustering up some reserve bravado she hadn't known she'd had, Sherri faced her father and Lynn with an angelic smile. "You must be tired, after all."

"Ah, well, okay." Sherri's dad seemed surprised. But Sherri didn't miss the speculative look that gleamed in Lynn's eyes for a moment. The woman was no fool, Sherri realized as she made an abrupt exit for the safety of the kitchen. There, she found both boys more than a little disgusted with her for maneuvering them into the kitchen. "What did you have to do this for?" Kyle snapped the dishtowel at her. "Tonight of all nights we could have gotten out of it."

"Well, just like I said. Lynn's probably tired. We can do it faster anyway, since we're used to it."

"You're a case, girl," Shane said shortly as he set down another big stack of dishes for her to rinse. "Half the evening you act like you don't care if she and Dad dropped off the edge of the earth, and then you're all worried about the dumb dishes."

"You're imagining things."

"I am not. You don't know whether you're coming or going."

"Right now, you're going to be going—out of here, if you don't get a move on." Sherri gave the brisk order from a sense of habit, thrusting a dishcloth into his hand. "Here, you wash. It'll give you something to do with your mind besides dream up dumb ideas."

"Don't get bossy. You're retired, remember?" Shane took the dishcloth, nevertheless.

"And you never had any rank in here in the first place," Sherri retorted. "So hush up and wash."

He muttered something under his breath that Sherri couldn't quite catch. She went to get the last of the things from the dining room, pausing on the other side of the doorway long enough to hear him grumble to Kyle, "Sometimes she is an absolute loon. It actually makes me worry for her."

Sherri sighed, scooping up the soiled napkins and rings. He just might be right, at that. How could she resent what he said when she, herself, wasn't sure what was going on in her own mind?

Chapter Five

It wasn't long before Sherri realized that life the way she'd known it was over. It didn't help anything that Kathleen arrived home from college just two days later. The ease with which the older girl seemed to blend into the ranch family grated on Sherri's nerves. She seemed as eager as her mother to make her presence felt and to know everything about everyone. And Sherri was beginning to see that even her months of scrambled thinking weren't going to begin to cover the multitude of ways in which they were all having to try to get used to each other.

Sherri'd been told she no longer had to worry about many of the things that had been her responsibilities: constant surveillance of Tim and Todd; planning meals and leaving notes for Mrs. Andersen; making lunches for those who carried their lunches to school; and many of the general housecleaning duties. But she quickly realized that it wasn't going to be quite that clean-cut. Lynn was too unfamiliar with the routine of the ranch. Even the short quantities at a few of the first meals vouched for her inexperience with a big family.

Sherri's father had mentioned only a certain number of specific things to her in redefining her duties. The problem was that there were still a lot of other things that she'd always done, just by default. She'd often wondered if their male clan was actually a bunch of closet-believers in evolution. They never seemed to give a thought to why certain household items reappeared in their correct places after being left at the barn or under the back porch. And not one of her brothers ever seemed to wonder why the supplies in the refrigerator and cupboards apparently grew up fresh from the shelf linings after having been consumed in a midnight raid.

But since her father hadn't seemed to think about it, and since Sherri would rather have done anything else than to have brought up the subject with Lynn, she was repeatedly jolted that first week by finding her stepmother in the middle of something that she'd always done: updating the grocery list for Mrs. Andersen or signing the little boys' homework assignments. Again and again Sherri backed off and said "Oh, that's fine—fine. Whatever." But then Saturday morning came, and their paths crossed again. This time it wasn't "fine."

Sherri had tumbled out of bed at about seven o'clock, which was normal for her as opposed to five o'clock on week days. During the school year they were all allowed to sleep later on Saturdays and Sundays. The ranch hands took care of the morning chores on those days, by decree of her father. Still, there were many things to be done on Saturday that made the rest of the week livable—cleaning of bedrooms, vacuuming, changing bed sheets, laundry, and other odds and ends.

No one was around when Sherri grabbed a granola bar and a glass of milk from the kitchen. Shane and Terry were probably already gone, she thought. Terry would be at the library in town most of the day, studying for finals next week. Shane had graduation rehearsal today. Kyle, Todd, and Tim, she supposed, were still in bed.

Oh well, I can get a start before they get up. Maybe I'll have time to take a ride up to Crest Spring this afternoon, she thought. It was beautiful up there in the spring. The water levels were high, and spunky young calves and colts were everywhere. There would be endless material for sketches.

Sherri was already mapping out some sketches in her mind as she pulled the sheets off her own bed. She carried them into the hall and dumped them into a pile outside the door of the bathroom at the end of the hall. There was a large laundry hamper there, complete with wheels. Sherri brought it into the hall, added the sheets, and proceeded to the next bathroom, where the hamper was a pull-out one from the counter. Finally, with a skyscraper load, she wheeled the whole mess down the long hall and through the kitchen to the laundry room.

She had the first load of towels running and was sorting the rest when she heard voices in the kitchen. Straightening up slightly, she listened for a moment. "Todd!" she called. "Come here for a minute, please."

A quick patter of feet answered. "What?" He stuck his dark head around the corner of the door. Sherri noted that he was still in his pajamas.

"As soon as you guys finish breakfast, you get the sheets off your beds, okay? And anything else from your room that needs to be washed."

He nodded slowly, looking a little puzzled—and that puzzled Sherri.

"Don't take forever about it, okay?" she chided from big-sister habit. "There's a lot to be done this morning. I want you guys to get your rooms straightened up and the trash down to the dumpster right away today—not halfway through the afternoon like last week. I want to take a ride up to Crest Spring today, and I can't go until you guys are finished."

Dead silence met her statement. Sherri looked up from emptying the pockets of a pair of blue jeans to see both Tim and Todd regarding her with long looks from the doorway. There was confusion and hesitation in their eyes. She hadn't noticed that Lynn was a few steps behind them. When Sherri straightened up, startled, she noticed that her stepmother was dressed to go out.

"Sherri." Lynn hesitated. "I'm so sorry. I had told them that I would take them into Riverton to see the AKC show today. They wanted to see the German shepherd classes, and those start at nine."

"The what?" Sherri knew what she meant, but surprise jolted the response from her anyway. The American Kennel Club was holding a large show in Riverton, a nearby town, this weekend.

"I didn't realize there were things they normally did on a Saturday morning." Lynn's words came a little slowly and unevenly, as though she wasn't terribly sure of what to say. "We'll just have to make sure we get back in time for them to get things done this afternoon."

Two bright smiles broke over two little faces. "All right!" they exclaimed in unison. Taking Lynn completely at her word—and not even waiting for Sherri's response—they turned from the doorway and charged away, their running footsteps rattling the pots in the kitchen cupboards.

Sherri stood, transfixed, limply holding Terry's jeans. She met her stepmother's eyes in frank amazement, expecting her to retract her words. No one was ever allowed to go anywhere or do anything before regular work had been taken care of.

When Sherri realized there was no apology or even recognition of wrong in Lynn's eyes, she felt the anger boil up. Turning abruptly away, she hurled the jeans into the pile of "darks" and went to the washer to add fabric softener to the rinse cycle for the towels. Her hands shook, causing her to spill the lemon-scented liquid onto her hand.

"Sherri?" Lynn sounded uncertain. "Is this going to cause problems for you?"

"Yes." Sherri said shortly, wiping her hand on the loose tail of Shane's old flannel shirt that she wore.

"Oh, dear." A long pause. "Why don't you just put off what you're doing and come with us? Then we can all work together to get things done when we get back."

"I don't think so. Dad would flip. Last time we skipped Saturday's jobs, we couldn't find the kitchen table by Tuesday.

That's just the way things are with a houseful—and we do laundry for the ranch hands too."

"Your father—" Lynn didn't have a chance to say more than the two words before Sherri cut her off.

"Besides, I don't want to. I have plans of my own this afternoon. So if you'll excuse me, I have a lot to do, I guess." Sherri brushed by her stepmother without looking at her and swiftly left the kitchen.

Sherri was dragging out the vacuum when Todd and Tim emerged, dressed and ready to go. They shot past her without so much as a second glance. "Bye, Sherri! See you later!"

Sherri didn't answer. She plugged the vacuum in and set to work with a fury, forgetting that Kyle was still asleep. She'd worked her way the length of the hall, through her own room and through Shane and Terry's when she heard him pass by the doorway, grumbling on his way to the shower. A glance at her watch said it was not yet 8:30.

"Oh, well," she said aloud, "that's the breaks today, buddy." Sherri was through all the rest of the bedrooms except his by the time Kyle reappeared. They met in the doorway to his room. She flicked the switch off and straightened to face him as the motor whined to a halt.

"Why didn't you just start at five?" Kyle was always a grouch in the mornings.

"Sorry. I forgot."

"I bet."

"I did! Besides, it looks like we both have extra to do today. Lynn just took Todd and Tim to the Riverton AKC show."

"She what? I mean, why?" Kyle frowned. "I didn't hear anything about that."

"Neither did I, but they left half an hour ago. The boys didn't do a thing before they left."

"Not even the trash?" Kyle would obviously take a special interest in this, since he knew that he'd have to do it if they didn't. All the trash at the ranch was hauled to the dump site several miles away each Saturday afternoon. That meant that all the trash in the house and in the outside dumpster had to be taken down to the main one by the barn—on time—so that Dandy, one of the ranch hands, could make it to the dump before it closed.

"Nope. Not even the trash." Sherri jerked the cord out from under the edge of the vacuum where it had caught. "Peachy, hmm?"

"Does Dad know about this?"

"I don't know. If he does, I bet he thinks they finished their stuff last night. Not to mention that I don't think either of them knows his verses for tomorrow."

"That's not going to go over real big," Kyle said thoughtfully.

"Tell me about it."

"Did you tell Lynn that?"

"No. It wasn't like she was asking my permission. It was more like, 'This is the way it is. So sorry, but goodbye.' "

"And you're mad." Kyle made it a statement rather than a question. He rarely got upset over anything.

"Yes, I am. You know who'll catch it if we have another scene over memory verses."

"Yeah."

"Well, tough. I'll just tell him what happened. I have the whole section for this quarter done, so I'm not going to worry about it." Sherri turned the vacuum on again and started across Kyle's room, drowning out any possible response. The conversation didn't pick up again until she was back in the laundry room, changing one load for another and loading the dryer.

Kyle came to the door, carrying a bowl of dry cereal which he munched on busily. "Why don't you like her, Sherri?"

The question caught Sherri off guard. "What makes you think I don't?" She needed a moment to think.

"Well, you don't act like it. I don't mean about this morning. But just generally. You hardly even talk to her."

"That's ridiculous. She's been here only five days."

"Yeah, I know. But still."

"You're imagining things, Kyle." Sherri knew that he most certainly wasn't, but there was no way she could explain to him how she felt around Lynn. Her uneasiness with her brother was a strange feeling in itself, because she'd always thought of Kyle as her best friend—the way she'd always assumed other girls must feel about their next-door best friends in books that she had read. Rockview was a little isolated for that, but Sherri had never felt shortchanged. Until now.

Now she desperately needed some input from someone who understood what she was feeling, but that was the problem. No one did. Sherri wasn't even sure she understood it herself. She knew the boys were all pleased to have Lynn around. It was a plus for them. It just made things easier and provided a lot of extras that they hadn't had before. But Sherri felt that the worst of her problems from school had come home to live with her. No longer did the ranch feel like a haven, even after a full day with her classmates.

It was nearly noon by the time Kyle and Sherri finished the things that needed to be done. The last load of clothes that couldn't go in the dryer hung on the drying rack on the back patio. The beds were made up with fresh sheets, floors vacuumed, bathrooms cleaned, trash dealt with, clean clothes put away, both patios swept, dusting done, and rooms straightened. That was the usual Saturday morning (or Friday night) routine, but normally it didn't take this long.

Since Saturday was also considered a fend-for-yourself lunch day, they grabbed quick sandwiches and headed their different directions. Kyle, the bookworm, was back in his room, sandwich and all, to take up where he'd left off the night before. Sherri grabbed a sketch pad compact enough to stuff in a saddle bag, and she headed for the barn.

Taffy was eager to go, and they made good time on the ride to Crest Spring. It was the time of year for everything to smell fresh and damp. Everywhere Sherri looked, things were budding and growing. The grass was more than just a green tint on the slopes now. It was an unbroken carpet, waving in the breeze. In the higher country, the leaves were still just a spray in the groves of aspen. The trails through the benches and parks were still sodden from the spring rains and from the melting snows that poured into overflowing creek beds from the snowcaps above.

Sherri lay on her back near the foaming jet of water that poured out from the canyon wall. Crest Spring. What an appropriate name, she thought, staring up at the slate blue peaks that towered above the valley. Had she been sitting, she could have looked down from the spring into the north end of the valley where the ranch buildings were. They couldn't quite be seen from here, but a little farther up the valley, they were visible from the trail that ran along the edge of a hundred-foot sheer drop. At that distance, the huge main barn appeared the size of a dime. The height was dizzying, even to someone accustomed to it.

Sherri never stopped feeling the impact of the size of the Rocky Mountains. Every time she rode into them or looked up at them, they made her feel insignificant and tiny. They were vast, intricate mazes of valleys and hidden canyons, stands of rustling aspen trees and an occasional dark spruce, and endless slopes that reached above and below her for miles farther than she could see. The air was fresh, cold, and thin, often hurting Sherri's lungs when she gasped for breath at the high altitude. On a cloudy day, the peaks couldn't be seen—not even from this valley. The normal height of the clouds hung them far below the jagged peaks.

On a clear day, it was evident even to a casual observer where the timber line ended and the barren tumble of rock and flint took over. Higher and higher those impassable cliffs rose, contrasting their grayishness against the brighter blue of the sky, until they ended in startling white—the ever-present snow that remained twelve months of the year.

I wish I had a good camera, Sherri thought, as she sat up and critically surveyed the sketch in her lap. Drawings were one thing, and even professional paintings another. But, somehow they just didn't quite do the trick. Sherri craned her neck upward again at the thousands of shades of variation in color and texture all around her.

Never in a million years, she thought dismally, getting up to stuff the sketch pad back into her saddlebag. A picture would have to be better. But she remembered, too, the poor results when she'd once brought her camera up to try to get a couple of shots. In spite of her past disappointment with the results, she had to laugh at the memory of those pieces of glossy paper that showed little or no resemblance to the beautiful Rockies.

When she returned from her ride, she felt considerably less tense. The mountains usually had that effect on her, and she knew that the physical exercise helped too. It was nearly dinner time. She knew she'd be expected to be there on time, so she hustled to get Taffy cared for and put away. She went in the end door, by her bedroom, pulling her boots off before she entered. After a quick wash-up, she made her way toward the kitchen, planning on snitching a Coke and some cookies before supper. Even though the weather was still comparatively cool, the dryness of the mountain air created an intense thirst.

As she neared the kitchen, Sherri stopped abruptly. Todd's voice came to her through the door and hallway.

"I don't want to!" The tone was an actual whine. "I did it last week. Make Tim do it."

"No!" The younger boy's response was equally nasal. "I'm hungry. I want to eat supper!"

Instantly Sherri realized that they were talking about filling the woodbox by the den fireplace.

"Boys, please." Lynn sounded weary. "If you'll both get started, it'll be done in a few quick minutes."

"Tim, you have to!" Todd was obviously relishing the thought of pushing the job off on his little brother.

"I do not! You didn't—"

"You do too!"

"I do not!"

EVERY PERFECT GIFT

As Sherri listened to Lynn try unsuccessfully to break in on them, she felt a surge of satisfaction. You might know a lot, Sherri's thoughts said to Lynn, but you've obviously never had little boys before. The decibel level increased rapidly, the words getting less intelligible by the second. The sounds of a physical scuffle started, punctuated by Lynn's short cry of frustration.

"Boys! Stop, now. This instant!"

Sherri was one step away from being actually amused when another thought struck. Her father would be in from the barn any minute. The house—Sherri included—would shake to the very foundations if he walked in on a scene like this. A few quick steps put Sherri into the kitchen.

"Todd! Tim!" Her voice snapped out. There was an abrupt, momentary silence. The scuffling stopped.

"Sherri, it's his turn to fill—"

"Quiet! Not another word from either of you!"

"But he—" Tim started, quickly breaking off as Sherri took a step toward him. He backed up, but she didn't stop. Sherri grabbed them each by a shoulder and spun them toward the screen door.

"You've got fifteen minutes, starting now, to have that woodbox filled and be washed up for supper. If I hear one word from either of you in the meanwhile, you'll have a spanking instead of supper. Now move!"

The boys rushed for the door. Sherri bit her lip speculatively and swung around to face Lynn. There was a direct challenge in the look she gave her stepmother.

But once again the surprise was Sherri's. She was embarrassed to see Lynn's dark eyes fill rapidly with tears. Fatigue was evident in every line of the woman's face. She must have had quite a day, Sherri realized. The boys would have been quick to capitalize on anything they thought they were going to get away with—probably from the moment she cancelled the morning chores.

Sherri opened and shut her mouth a couple of times. A second before, there'd been a dozen things she'd wanted to say. But once again, the strange sense of uneasiness robbed her of words. Not knowing what was expected of her, and being pretty sure that she wouldn't have done it anyway, Sherri simply turned away and left the room without a word.

She joined the family at the dinner table an hour later, trying to anticipate whether Lynn would be moody and quiet or would retaliate by bringing the whole day out in the open to her husband. To Sherri's surprise, her stepmother did neither. Though she looked a little tired, Lynn was as soft-spoken and cheerful as ever, inquiring about Terry's upcoming exams and asking whether Shane was ready with his salutatorian's speech for tomorrow's graduation ceremony.

Sherri chewed on a piece of garlic bread and said nothing. Who is she trying to impress? she wondered. She already has Dad. Or doesn't she have any feelings of her own?

Todd and Tim were silent throughout the meal. Their occasional glances at Sherri let her know they were in terror that she would recount the earlier scene to their father. Sweat it out, chums, she said inwardly. We're all stuck with her, but there's no way I'm going to let you guys get me in trouble over her foul-ups.

Chapter Six

Sherri sat in the fold-down chair of the school auditorium and tried to pull herself up into the smallest amount of space possible. Unconsciously, she was rolling the corner of the graduation program back and forth. To both sides of her, animated conversation was going on among her family members. Even Uncle Henry and Aunt Maud, her mother's brother and his wife, were here from Colorado, having arrived late the night before.

Sherri had always enjoyed their company, but she'd been unable to get much pleasure from their visit so far. With Lynn and Kathleen involved in every conversation and seeming to fit in with the greatest of ease and enjoyment, it didn't even feel like home anymore in the big stone ranch house.

Sherri consoled herself with the thought that neither one of them was going to be worth a dime for ranch work. They'd proven that earlier in the week. Sherri had wondered about it just a little, because Lynn and Kathleen both said that they'd done a fair bit of riding. However, the first thirty seconds—seeing them mount—told her all she needed to know. They managed all right, but both sat their horses like sacks of potatoes: heels up and reins long. Completely typical of Easterners who say that they can ride, Sherri thought with a twinge of satisfaction.

She saw Terry's thin-lipped smile and heard him mutter "First class pair of dudes." There was no malice in his remark, but it pleased Sherri to hear him say it.

Shane caught the comment though, and his response annoyed her. "With a girl as pretty as that, who cares how she rides?" He whispered the remark from behind Sherri and walked away. She didn't favor him with any sort of answer, but his words bit hard. Especially now as she sat in the auditorium with the pair of them right beside her.

Kathleen kept peppering her with questions about the school, various students, and the graduation ceremony. Sherri hated to answer at all. She kept her responses to a minimum, pretending to be deeply absorbed in the program she held, though its corner was disintegrating into shreds. What a contrast we must make, Sherri thought. Beauty and the beast, or something like that.

If she just wasn't so friendly, Sherri thought. She must be used to new people and new places. Kathleen's father had been in the Air Force, and the family had spent most of their lives moving around—Tom Merriell had been killed in a car accident less than two years ago. The apparent result of all that traveling around was a daughter who didn't seem to recognize a rebuff when she received one. Just yesterday she'd wandered into Sherri's room while Sherri was sprawled on her bed cramming for her geometry exam.

"Hi. Sorry. I hope I'm not intruding. I'm just looking around and trying to get acquainted."

Sherri thought she ought to realize that she obviously was intruding, but couldn't quite bring herself to say so. As usual, she said nothing. Kathleen didn't seem to notice. She walked to the opposite wall and stood admiring the range of trophies and ribbons that lined one shelf.

"Are these all yours?"

"No, I stole them." Sherri tossed out the flippant reply in annoyance. What a dumb question.

Kathleen just laughed. "What are they from? They don't look like anything I recognize."

"Probably not. They're from speed contests, mostly. And some cutting horse events."

"Speed contests?"

"Yeah. Like short races, but you have to do things during the race. Pick up and drop a few flags, or run in a certain pattern, or pick somebody else up on your horse or something."

"And the cutting—is that what you called it?"

"Cutting horses are horses that work with cattle."

"You must be awfully good." Kathleen turned around and stared at Sherri curiously.

"The guys are lots better." Sherri shrugged. "But I have a faster horse. It evens out."

"Your brothers, you mean?"

Sherri nodded. She wondered if this girl was just out of touch or actually a little slow on the uptake. Kathleen's next question made her realize what she'd been hinting at, though.

"Are there other girls that ride in these events?"

Sherri actually rolled over on the bed to face her better. She squinted carefully at the older girl but couldn't quite read her expression. "Yeah. Lots of them. Why?"

"Oh, just curious." Kathleen beat a hasty retreat and changed the subject. "I saw your brothers loading their horses on a trailer a little while ago. What were they up to? One of these contests you're talking about?"

"Hardly." Sherri slammed her book shut and pushed herself up off the bed. "Not this time of year. They're going up to the north end of the ranch to do some separating work."

"To the—but I thought there was going to be a big drive sometime next week."

"There will be. They're getting ready for it."

"But why. . . . " Kathleen's voice trailed away. She frowned in confusion. "The trailer, I mean."

Sherri realized what was puzzling her. "Oh. I see what you mean." She laughed, in spite of herself, as she explained shortly. "These days, the horses are needed for the work with the cattle, not for transportation. Sometimes, like when you're actually moving big herds or when you're going way up in the range where there aren't any roads, you have to ride the horses all the way up. But whenever possible, you take the horses to the cattle with a trailer. It saves your time and their energy."

The familiar strains of "Pomp and Circumstance" jolted Sherri back to the auditorium as long lines of cap-and-gowned graduates came down the aisles. Pretty soon it's going to be me, she thought uneasily. What then? College of course. But *what* in college? Could she really survive a college art program? Sherri had no idea. What if she couldn't make it? Would she face a lot of I-told-you-so's and ridicule? She tightened her grip on the arms of her seat. Her thoughts edged closer to an area that she usually preferred to ignore. How different would it be if Mom was still alive? She couldn't help wondering, though she rarely permitted herself to think about it. One thing's for sure, she told herself, I wouldn't be sitting here beside these two.

The program seemed endless as award after award was presented and graduate after graduate made his speech. The only one Sherri heard was Shane's. She was proud that he was salutatorian, but his cocky assurance grated on her raw nerves as he spoke with confidence about his plans for the future and how well prepared he felt he was.

Kathleen stirred slightly, sending a whiff of her perfume wafting across Sherri. She couldn't keep herself from glancing sideways at the neat linen suit that the older girl wore. Is she an example of what I have to face in college? Sherri wondered. The thought wasn't encouraging. She felt herself close to tears as the recessional music began.

Snap out of it, she rebuked herself as she watched for her brother's face in the procession. But she couldn't shake the feeling that things were moving too fast for her to keep up with, much less control.

School closed four days later, and in spite of her discomfiture at the ranch, Sherri felt as though someone had rolled a ton of bricks from her shoulders. A whole glorious summer stretched ahead of her. Days would be filled with things that she enjoyed and could do with competence. And to make it even better, Kathleen was leaving for a couple of weeks. She was going to visit a friend in California. Sherri hoped that Kathleen's time away would give her a chance to get adjusted to Lynn's presence a little better. That failing, it wouldn't be any worse than having the two of them there.

That week, however, the Rockview schedule picked up to a pace about one step short of panic. The spring roundup was at hand—and overdue. Normally it was done before school was out, but spring weather had been late to arrive this year. Now Dad said it couldn't be put off for even another week.

So all hands and family members scrambled to get things ready. The herds in the home pastures had to be sorted and separated: some to sell, some to keep here, some to drive up to the summer pasture. There were medical work, marking, weighing, record-keeping, and pasture shuffling to be done. Then the drive itself would occupy several days and involve most of the ranch hands as well as the James family.

Time flew by, and suddenly it was almost time to go. Sherri was thinking out the schedule as she helped with one of the last separating projects. Tomorrow the trucks come to pick up the sale stock, she told herself. The day after that, we go.

"There's another one, Sherri!" Kyle's voice snapped her out of her daydreaming.

Sherri reined Taffy in and turned to look where Kyle was pointing. Sure enough. There was another yearling heifer burrowing her way into the center of the adult herd.

"Rats. How did I miss her?" Sherri muttered as she nudged Taffy back into the group. They sidled up to the nervous animal, and Sherri pressed a leg against Taffy's side. The cream-colored mare whirled around and began forcing the heifer out of the herd, step by step. Back and forth, forward and back, with 180-degree spins and sliding stops. The dust flew as the heifer was driven back toward the end of the ring.

"Sherri!"

She noticed Shane just across the rail.

"Hey! Get a rope on her! She's a slick!"

He meant that there was no brand on the young cow. That was unusual, but not unheard of. In the rush and fuss of branding the previous spring, they must have overlooked one. Sherri couldn't see well enough to get a good look, but she knew Shane could see better from where he was.

Sherri grabbed the lariat from its hitch and expertly played it out into a loop. Swinging it a couple times to clear any possible snarls, Sherri made a slight gesture with the reins to check Taffy to a halt and spin her to face away from the heifer. As the little animal came charging from behind to rejoin the herd, she flicked the loop over it and did a quick hitch around Taffy's saddle horn.

When the heifer hit the end of the rope, Taffy automatically sat back, yanking in the slack. Sherri dismounted, knowing that the mare would keep it that way. Shane vaulted over the fence. He had a tie cord in one hand and a bottle of branding fluid in the other. He tossed Sherri the fluid and made short work of throwing and tying the calf. He held the animal steady while Sherri applied the fluid in the familiar pattern of the R and crest that was the Rockview trademark.

It would take a few minutes to dry, so Shane stayed where he was. Sherri stood up and walked back to her horse. At Sherri's signal, Taffy slacked up on the rope immediately. The heifer lunged, but Shane held her. Sherri pulled the lariat off and began recoiling it. Only then did she notice that Kathleen was leaning on the fence railing, watching closely.

"Hi." Sherri hadn't known she was there. "I didn't see you before. I thought you'd be getting ready to go. Don't you leave tonight?"

"Yes, but I felt like a walk, so I came down to see what was going on. Everybody else is down here."

"Umm-hmm. Dad wants to push most of the stock up to the summer range in a couple days, so there's a lot to do if we expect to get it done before the weekend." Sherri refastened the rope to her saddle. It seemed strange. This was the only place where she ever felt she was on equal footing with Kathleen. Well, maybe not so strange. At least she didn't have as much trouble thinking of something to say.

"Is that the horse you won all the trophies with?" Kathleen seemed genuinely interested. Sherri made an effort to be at least somewhat friendly.

"Yes and no. Some of them." She led Taffy toward Kathleen. "This is Taffy. She's the one that accounts for the cutting classes and the form contests, like reining, working cow horse, trail classes, and stuff like that. But the barrel and pole races are no good for a horse that's as well trained as she is. I use my gelding, Sprint, for those."

"He's not well trained then?"

"Not like Taffy. He knows the race patterns, sure, and he's really good at that. But all he knows is running, and he's kind of a feather-brain. He's worse than useless for any kind of ranch work, but he'd murder Taffy in an out-and-out race."

"Hmm."

"Sprint is over there." Sherri pointed to the corral where the black gelding stood dozing by the water trough. "He doesn't look very lively right now, but his whole personality changes when you put a saddle on him."

"Hey, you guys! Hurry up!" Terry was yelling from the main barn door. "We've got to get the bunch from the west field cut before supper!"

Kyle and Sherri scrambled to swing the partition gates shut in the middle of the corral, leaving the little heifer nowhere to go but to join the herd in the next pen as Shane pulled the tie rope off. Bawling her annoyance, she trotted away.

When Sherri returned to Taffy, Lynn had joined Kathleen at the fence.

"You're really good at this stuff, aren't you, Sherri?" Kathleen seemed a little confused, but Sherri couldn't figure out exactly why. She didn't know what to answer—nor did she know that Kyle was right behind her and had heard the question.

"You bet she is. Dad always says she's worth two hired hands on a job or a drive. And she's a better roper than even Shane and Terry. Like on the drive this week. Dad would have to have outside help if she couldn't go."

"Are you going, Sherri?"

Sherri could hear the surprise in Lynn's quick question.

"Sure. I always do." Sherri grinned, partly in amusement at the response and partly in anticipation of the upcoming event. "This is the most beautiful time of the year in the high country. And the drive is a two or three night camp-out trip by the time everything's done. Absolutely gorgeous up there in the spring! Even if there's a lot of work." Sherri stopped for a moment, thinking of the towering, snow-capped peaks standing bare above the high parklands of dark, evergreen spruce and fluffy, light green cottonwoods. Down in the canyons and bottoms of the bright green ridges, between the croppings of flint rock, the sparkling streams would still be cold enough to float ice. They were constantly fed, all summer long, by the drifts of snow that lay above the timber line. Sherri's thoughts wandered briefly as she wondered whether she should try to bring her camera along again. Someday she might get lucky and get a good shot.

"But don't you—" Sherri didn't miss Lynn's restraining hand on Kathleen's arm as the phrase broke off. "Well, I mean, it seems like you'd have to be twice as good as the guys to be able to hold your own. You're about half their size."

Sherri turned away, checking Taffy's girth. "A lot of it's not a question of strength." She mounted quickly. "It's just knowing what you're doing. I have to go." She tightened her legs and Taffy sprang into a lope.

Sherri tried to unclench her jaw and smooth out the frown on the way to the far corrals. "She's probably never worked a day in her life, Taffy," Sherri informed her mare. "Who does she think she is to be so superior?"

Sherri knew full well what the other girl had been about to say. Something about the dirt and mess, or else all the roughness. Kathleen had been wearing the same expression that she'd shown a few days before when she'd asked whether or not other girls competed in the speed contests.

Sherri couldn't seem to find an outlet for her frustration that day, as she usually could. Even the hot, pressured work of the rest of the afternoon couldn't drive her mind from the distaste she'd heard in Kathleen's voice. It embarrassed her in a way and made her mad at the same time. But this is new to her too, Sherri thought, trying to find a way to be fair about it. Maybe I'm as upsetting to them as they are to me. Once we all adjust to the ways that the others are used to living, things will tone down a little.

A shower and dinner seemed like a long time coming that night. It was after nine o'clock when Sherri finally collapsed in her room. She was ready to crawl into bed when she decided that a last glass of lemonade would be a great idea. She stuffed her feet back into her slippers and went out to the kitchen.

She was surprised to see her father sitting at the kitchen table. He was leaning back in his chair, feet propped on another chair nearby. He'd apparently thought more lemonade was a good idea, too, because he held a half-empty glass in his hand.

"Thought you were in bed, Sherri." He swiveled the ice cubes in his glass.

"Almost, but not quite." She smiled as she pulled a glass from the cupboard and went to the refrigerator. "I needed to have a last try at washing the dust out of my throat."

"Yeah." He continued sloshing the ice cubes around while she poured herself a glass and took a long drink.

"Well." She gave the refrigerator door an extra push. It was getting so it didn't want to close right. "Bed is where I'm headed. I'll see you in—"

"Sherri." Her father closed his eyes as he spoke, then reopened them. "Sit down for a minute, will you?" He pushed another chair away from the table with his foot.

"Sure." Stifling a yawn and a frown of puzzlement together, she slid into the seat.

"Sherri, I, ah, don't know exactly how to say this." Her dad swung his feet down with a thump and heaved a big sigh. "Both because I know you aren't going to like it and because it goes against what I want and need personally, but I know it's right."

Sherri made no attempt to keep the frown away this time. What in the world was he talking about? Maybe it was just too late and he was just too tired to be making much sense.

"I've been talking with Lynn tonight, and she's reminded me—well, no maybe I should say she made me realize something." He paused for a long moment. "Sherri, you're no kid anymore. You're an up-and-coming young lady. That's something I tend to overlook just because to me it seems you ought to be about ten years old yet. But you're not. And. . . ."

His voice trailed off. He looked at her, looked away, looked back, and looked away again. Raking his fingers through his hair, he thumped his hand on the table. "Honey, there's just no way you belong on a four-day cattle drive with a bunch of cowhands. You're worth more than 'most three of 'em put together, but it's not good for you to be up there as the only girl—and I think that's just where we're going to have to leave it from now on."

If he'd have slapped her across the face, Sherri couldn't have been any more shocked—or hurt. She opened her mouth to say something. Anything. But nothing would come. It was a full fifteen seconds before she could find her voice. "Dad! I've always gone! I'm not doing anything wrong!"

"I know that, Sherri. But you're sixteen years old, and I don't want you spending the rest of your life thinking you're one of the ranch hands. I've made the decision, and you're going to have to accept it as final. You are not going with us anymore."

"This is all Lynn's idea, isn't it?" Sherri knew better than to raise her voice, but all of a sudden she felt the heat flush clear to her hairline, and she couldn't help herself. Pushing her chair back from the table, she went to the sink. With shaking hands, she dumped the rest of the lemonade down the drain. "What's the matter, Dad?" Sherri whirled back to face him. "Isn't she content to make me feel like an idiot here in the house? Can't she take it that there's something I can do better than her?"

"That's enough!" Her dad was on his feet, too.

"You bet it is!" The tears were threatening to choke off her voice. "I've had enough of her! She can't just butt in and try to rearrange my life to suit herself! There's a lot of things about her I don't like either, but I'm not trying to make her change! I—"

"Quiet!" Her father's voice cut her off. "I will not tolerate this from you, young lady!" He took a step toward her, looking like a huge thundercloud.

The tears finally spilled over. Sherri wouldn't even look at him.

"You will do as I say, and there'll be no more—"

Sherri turned, ducked past him, and walked out of the room.

"Sherri!"

Sherri figured that anyone in the next county could have heard him. Rather than stop, Sherri fled to her room at top speed, slammed the door, flicked off the light, and threw herself on the bed.

A moment later she heard his footsteps coming down the hall. She knew she was in for it, but even that didn't quell the huge waves of resentment that were churning inside her. Just before he reached the door, she heard a soft voice that she recognized as Lynn's.

She couldn't make out the words, but the footsteps stopped. The murmur came again.

"No!" That was her father again. "I'll not have—"

"If you'll" . . . murmur, murmur, "be even what" . . . murmur, murmur "needs to."

A huge sigh from her father.

"Okay?"

His response dropped so far in volume that Sherri could barely pick it up. "I'm too old to be a father. Or too young. Or something."

Sherri flung herself over on her back, too angry to really cry. She listened as their footsteps receded. She could feel herself shaking, and her jaw hurt from being clenched so hard. Who did she think she was? Even Lynn's obvious interference on Sherri's behalf did nothing but make her angry. Did she figure she could have everything the way she wanted it? Everything to suit herself? It was none of her business! Why couldn't she just leave well enough alone? A thousand questions played over and over in Sherri's mind and made her want to shout, "She had no right! No right at all!"

Chapter Seven

The next morning Sherri woke up in a mood for trouble. The room was still dark, and a glance at her alarm clock told her that no one else would be up yet. Quietly she slipped from her bed and made her way to the shower. Fifteen minutes later, she was padding to the kitchen in her stocking feet. There she poured a large paper cup of milk and left the house for the barn.

On the patio, she stopped to pull on her boots. A faint pink hue was lighting the sky to the east. Sherri hustled along. She knew she didn't have much time before others would be up and about. The only legitimate excuse she could think of to get away from the house was that she hadn't ridden Tramp, the young gelding, in two days. He could use a long workout.

In a matter of minutes, Sherri had roped him in from the corral, groomed and saddled him, and mounted. She had just turned him to circle the barn and enter the north pasture when she heard a voice behind her.

"Where ya going, Sherri?"

Sherri turned in her saddle to see the curious face of their weather-bronzed ranch foreman. "Hi, Luke. I'm going to take Tramp up to some of the high trails and see how he acts. Dad's going to want to sell him soon."

Luke frowned. "There's a passle of stuff to be done here today, Sher. Did yer dad okay this? Don't forget we're supposed to leave in the morning."

Sherri turned her back on the foreman. "I'm not going with you."

"You're what?"

Sherri didn't have to see his face to catch the surprise. "I said I'm not going!" Even as she said it, she regretted the sharpness in her voice. It wasn't his fault. But it's not mine either, she thought, surprising even herself with the force of her anger. Tramp shifted nervously beneath her, sensing her feelings in that uncanny way that horses do.

"See you later, Luke. Don't expect me back till afternoon."

"Sherri—" Whatever the foreman had been about to say, Sherri didn't wait to hear it. She tightened her legs, and Tramp moved away at a jog. Any minute now her father would be showing up, and she wasn't about to face him this morning if she could help it. She also knew that no one would be able to take the time to come after her today.

Three hours later, Sherri pulled Tramp to a stop near the mouth of Blind Valley. She let the tired gelding breathe for a few moments. She had pushed him hard. Her gaze wandered vacantly to the ancient split-rail fence that the nearby trees partially camouflaged. The fence spread out in wing formation from either side of the valley entrance. Years ago, it had been used as a wild horse trap. The valley looked wide and inviting from this end, but less than half a mile from the entrance, it curved around and narrowed sharply. There was a corral built across the far end, with a similar squeeze alley of split rails—much smaller—to force the horses in. It was a natural trap.

But its usefulness had pretty much ended many years ago with the national laws that now forbade most forms of corraling and removing herds of wild horses. Sherri viewed those policies with mixed emotions. There were few horses that she didn't like, and almost everybody loved the concept of wild horses running free and untamed. Everybody but the ranchers—and especially her dad. Rockview had its share of trouble with a stallion that ran loose on a nearby federal reserve.

Most of the wild horses today were scrubs—unattractive animals that were victims of inbreeding and poor living conditions. Land with much forage was almost always ranch land—and ranchers would turn themselves inside out to keep pesky horses from consuming valuable feed. Even if the horses could have been captured, their conformation and physical state was usually so poor that they wouldn't be worth a dime for ranch work or even as pleasure-riding horses.

Tell that to the politicians, Sherri thought. She knew that they answered to their voting public—the people who still cherished the wild horse as the romantic symbol of early America. Sherri often wondered if people even realized that horses were not native to the continent. Spanish conquistadors had introduced the horse to North America, bringing shiploads of them, most of Arabian and Andalusian breeding. "Feral" horses—escapees gone wild—soon roamed in the unsettled west. Food wasn't a problem, and unlimited space was a natural protection against the inbreeding that so quickly emphasizes a horse's faults. The herds grew and spread, constantly resupplied by more escaping animals. In those days, huge herds of wild horses were everywhere, beautiful and strong. But through the years, the settling of the land began the constant rancher-vs.-wild horse struggle.

Sherri gave herself a mental shake and jerked herself back to the present. She would go on up to Pine Bench and check their own herd of horses, as long as she was this close. Really, she knew that she was not acting in her own best interests. It was an unwritten rule of all ranches that you didn't ride this far alone, unless someone knew exactly where you planned to go and when to expect you back. Too many things could happen.

"Oh, well." She sighed. "Come on, Tramp. We'll go up to the spring and get you a drink." Sherri was vaguely aware that her stomach was rumbling, but her insides were so tied in knots that she knew she wouldn't have eaten if she had brought any food with her. A glance at her watch showed her that it was a little after nine a.m. But after a long, lingering stop at the Pine Bench Spring, an inspection of the ranch herd of retirees and young stock, and a slow retracing of her long route, it was 2:30 in the afternoon before she dismounted to let Tramp through the gate into the north pasture.

Sherri had walked him the last couple miles in, so his coat was no longer dark with sweat. But there was still a major grooming job ahead of her before she could turn him out. Sherri skirted the holding corrals where she could see that her family and the hands were finishing up the separating work for the morning's drive. She wasn't sure whether anyone had seen her come back, but she was about halfway through hosing Tramp off when she heard Shane's voice behind her.

"Where've you been, Sherri?"

She didn't have to turn her head far to see him standing in the side door of the barn, a shoulder propped against the wall.

"Out." She moved to Tramp's other side and began her work there.

Shane didn't say anything right away. He just picked up a metal scraper and came to join her. On the opposite side of the gelding, he began squeezing the excess water from the bay coat. Sherri didn't look at him. Anger was still churning around inside her. Not at him, really, but she was feeling basically hostile toward everyone that crossed her path. She'd finished with the hose and gone to the spigot to turn it off before Shane spoke again.

"Dad told us that he's not letting you go."

"Yeah."

"If it's any comfort, he's not mad at you for taking off today. He didn't say anything at all."

"I don't care if he's mad or not."

"Obviously." Shane moved to Tramp's other side. "Sherri, this isn't very easy for him either, you know."

Sherri didn't answer. She just began coiling up the hose, loop by loop, over the wide metal hanger.

"You're the only girl he has. And nobody ever did everything perfectly." Shane finished scraping, knocked the scraper against his boot to clear the hair, and turned to look at her. "If he had what he wanted, you'd be coming. But what he's doing, he's doing because he thinks it's best for you." Shane paused. "Besides. He's right."

Sherri grabbed a cloth and went back to Tramp, beginning the second step in drying him off. She still didn't say anything to her brother, but her motions with the cloth were abrupt and harsher than normal.

Shane stared at her for a long moment. "Personally, if I were him, I'd be tempted to bounce you off the wall once or twice."

Sherri suddenly realized that her clenched jaw was pushing her lip out in a very obvious gesture.

"It's not going to hurt you any to act more like a girl." Shane's voice grew hard. He started for the door. "Sometimes I wonder if you realize that's what you are. I meant it when I said I hoped Lynn would have a good effect on you—but you're obviously not going to let her."

Shane stopped in the doorway. He spoke with his back to her. "It's time to grow up, Sherri. At least a little. You're not a kid anymore." Then he was gone.

Trust Shane to be blunt, Sherri thought. Through the brain and out the mouth. That was the way he operated. As much as his words rankled in her mind, they just settled her more firmly on the idea that no one was going to force changes on her.

"They're just different from me, Tramp," Sherri told the gelding as she took him to the trough for a drink. "Things are different out here. Mom used to ride with Dad and the rest of them. He's told me that lots of times. Why should it be any different for me?"

The gelding raised his head and snorted, spraying her with water droplets. "Yuk!" Sherri objected, wiping her face with her sleeve. "Well, I don't care what you think, either. They can't force their way of life on me."

Sherri was still dwelling on that thought half an hour later. After a quick shower, she sat in her room at her desk with a huge sketch pad. Absently, she let her fingers trace out a thumbnail outline of the scenery and fence at the mouth of Blind Valley. Under her quickly moving pencil, the mountain slopes and aspen groves appeared, then the towering peaks, the waving grass, and the split-rail fence partially concealed by the trees. Finally, a horse and rider took form halfway across the entrance: an old-world cowboy from the era that made the West famous. The horse was small and wiry, the rider thin and slouched. He wore an oversized, broad-brimmed hat and thick leather chaps. Sherri was putting the finishing touches on the rope that hung from the saddle horn when a voice made her jump.

"Sherri, that's a wonderful drawing!"

Sherri jumped half out of her chair. In the same instant, she recognized Lynn's voice without turning around. Slamming the sketch pad shut, she stood up quickly, almost bumping the straight-backed chair into her stepmother. Sherri didn't apologize or even comment as she made her way to the large shelves on the other side of the room and returned the sketch pad to its usual place.

"I came to see if you'd be interested in going with us to pick up Tim's puppy."

Sherri knew that Tim and Todd, after the AKC show, had talked their father into letting them get another shepherd puppy on the reasoning that they needed a dog for each of them. Sherri couldn't quite agree that another dog underfoot was an urgent need just now, but recently it had been the least of her worries.

"No." She paused, still with her back to Lynn, uncertain where to go next. She stood with a hand pressed against her temple.

"I thought you'd enjoy seeing the kennels."

"No." Sherri repeated the monosyllable flatly. Suddenly she picked the sketch pad up again, dropped into the big rocker, and reopened the pad to the page she'd been working on.

"Tim wants you to go." Lynn's voice remained low and perfectly even.

Sherri didn't answer. Nor did she look up. Her pencil was busy where she'd left off, filling in the sketch with a few head of scruffy cattle.

"Sherri—" The inflection of the single word made it obvious that Lynn expected acquiescence or an explanation.

Sherri felt a flicker of perverse satisfaction as she kept her head bent over the sketch.

"All right, then." Lynn didn't seem about to give up. "I want you to go. I'm asking you to go."

Sherri felt a rush of anger. The pencil point snapped under the pressure she suddenly applied. "Well, I'm not going." She met her stepmother's eyes directly, letting all the hostility show as freely as she felt it. "Because I don't want to and I don't have to."

Sherri resisted the desire to look away from the level steadiness of the gaze that confronted her. Clenching her jaw, she forced herself to hold up her end of the stare down. She was almost ready to give up when Lynn turned away.

"Very well." Swiftly, the dark-haired woman left the room.

Chapter Eight

Certainly, having a dentist clean your teeth was nothing to get excited about, but Sherri felt that it beat being with Lynn. Anything did. By a long shot. The previous night—the night before everyone else left—Sherri's father had reminded her of the dentist's appointment. Their family car was in the garage. Dandy would be picking it up today, but meanwhile Lynn had to drive Sherri to her appointment.

Sherri closed her eyes and hoped that the woman doing the job would get the hint. The gritty, fake-strawberry goo in her mouth was bad enough without the running string of comments and questions.

Sherri could never figure out how they expected you to answer, anyway. If they really wanted you to say anything, they would have to stop what they were doing and get their hands out of your mouth so you could form words. It had always seemed like a pretty complete waste of time sitting in the dentist's office, chatting away and making the ordeal twice as long as necessary. Maybe, Sherri thought, they charge by the hour. That's why it's so expensive—and why they ask so many dumb questions.

At least there were no fillings necessary this time. That was some consolation. It wasn't the filling she dreaded, but spending the rest of the day with a saggy lip. She always worried that she should wear a drool bib.

Eventually, though, she had to return to the waiting room. Sherri paused before turning the knob and took a deep breath. Stepping out into the lounge area, she saw that Lynn was chatting away with a lady whom she didn't recognize. The stranger looked about fifty years old, but Sherri could practically feel her pep all the way across the room. Her jet-black hair was shot through with silver, almost a perfect match to her greyish tweed suit.

"Oh, there she is now." Lynn interrupted the woman. There was nothing for Sherri to do but walk over to them.

"This is Sherri James." Lynn spoke as smoothly as though there had never been an iota of disagreement between them. "Sherri, this is Mrs. Linda Vey. She is a dear friend of mine who works here in town. We were in college together—quite some time ago!"

"How do you do, Mrs. Vey?"

To her surprise, the woman stood up and extended her hand. "Very well, Sherri. Thank you."

Sherri gave a half-hearted handshake, not really sure what else she was supposed to say or do.

Mrs. Vey's smile was beautiful. Her eyes, dark as her hair, sparkled at Sherri as though they were sharing some secret.

"Lynn has just been telling me of your interest in artwork. It sounds as though you have some real aptitude."

"Oh." Sherri took a half-step back and laughed a little shortly. "I wonder exactly what she's been telling you, then."

Mrs. Vey's laugh was as clear as her voice. "Oh, my dear. I'm always interested in anyone who's interested in art. That's my field, you know. I work at the Krayfor Advertising Agency."

"Really?" Sherri couldn't keep the curiosity down. "My art class took a tour there once last year. That's a huge place. I loved seeing it."

"Hmm. You see, Lynn, I told you!" Mrs. Vey reached for her purse, then seemed to be talking to Sherri again. "I've not seen my old pal here in so long—I've been invited to dinner at your lovely ranch this evening, and I've been trying to convince Lynn that you would like to come back to the agency with me this afternoon and have a look around before going home."

Sherri knew her eyes answered for her before she could even say a word.

"Um-hmm. I thought so. Nothing is quite as dull as an afternoon of traipsing around town on someone else's errands."

True enough. But Mrs. Vey was missing the point. Sherri would have volunteered for a tour of an ostrich farm to get out of the ride back to the ranch with Lynn—but a chance to get inside the Krayfor agency again to boot! Mrs. Vey was already finalizing the matter.

"Lynn, my dear, you just run along, and we'll see you around five-thirty or six. All right?"

"Very well. Enjoy yourself, Sherri." Lynn's voice and composure gave no hint that she knew what her stepdaughter was thinking. But Sherri knew she did. She made no reply.

The trip to Krayfor was filled with questions—all from Mrs. Vey. "So you're going into your junior year?"

"Yes, ma'am."

"What art courses do they offer in your high school now?"

"Well, you can take art every year, if you want, but there's not really any distinction between the classes, other than the grade level of the students in them."

"I see. Do you cover the same material each year?"

"Some of it. We did some different things this last year than my first year. But the courses aren't really cumulative, either, because anyone can take art as a junior or senior when they haven't taken it before. See what I mean?"

"No specialized courses?"

"No, ma'am. Mr. Darrin was talking about offering a noncredit calligraphy course in the evenings next year, if he can get enough interest."

"Um-hmm. Do you intend to take that?"

"Well, I'd like to, but I doubt if it would work out for me to be running in and out of town much at night, at the distance we live. Plus, I'm needed there a lot."

"Yes." Mrs. Vey's answer was matter-of-fact, as though she were quite familiar with the situation. "But surely things are easier for you now that Lynn is there? It must give you more time to yourself."

Sherri almost choked on the hot words that wanted to leap out. It was a moment before she trusted herself to speak. "Sort of. But still. There's some things, well, like Todd and Timmy. They still need me a lot."

They had reached the multilevel parking garage. Mrs. Vey zipped right up to the fourth level. A parking slot with her name on it waited. Sherri had never been beyond the second level before, so it surprised her when they went across an enclosed walkway to the building across the street rather than taking the elevator down. The questions ceased, and Mrs. Vey began talking like a tour guide as they passed through double glass doors into a thickly carpeted hallway.

"This is the Spaldman Building, Sherri. Your class probably came in on the other side, and maybe didn't realize that. There are a number of different businesses that lease their office space from the Spaldman Company. Krayfor is just one of them."

Sherri was looking around at the various offices as they approached the elevators at a brisk pace.

"This floor is taken up mostly with individual law offices or CPAs or the like. The bank is on the first and second floors. We're on the ninth."

The moment they stepped out of the mirror-walled elevator, Sherri felt her heart rate increase. The large lobby was exactly as she remembered it. Thick, dusty-rose carpeting, dotted with furniture of a darker hue. A lot of glistening brass trim everywhere—even on the receptionist's glass-topped desk.

"Hello, Linda!" The girl behind the desk spoke cheerfully. "Your separations came in about an hour ago."

"Thank you. I'll see to them before I leave. This way, Sherri."

They whisked through the swinging doors behind the receptionist and made a right turn down a short hall into the art department. It too was as Sherri remembered it. The smells of paper, wax, and ink set her senses tingling. Gone was the neat, detailed order of the outer office. Here, everything was happy chaos. A dozen or more windowed offices opened onto the main floor, where a variety of extra work stations stood around. Paper cutters, supply cabinets, piles of scrap, and large, memo-and-photo-covered cork bulletin boards were everywhere.

Sherri felt her fingers itch for the materials that were just inches away. She stood and stared, drinking it all in, until she realized that Mrs. Vey was watching her with an amused expression. "The atmosphere appeals to you?"

Sherri flushed a little and nodded.

"Well, come. Let's give you a closer look."

For the next hour, they toured the department, meeting people and investigating the offices. For once, someone was willing to answer, in detail, the dozens of questions that swarmed through Sherri's mind. But the highlight came when they entered the darkroom.

"Color processing on this side, black and white over there, Sherri. The room for drying and trimming, as well as filing and storage, is just through there."

"Oh!" Sherri couldn't keep back the exclamation as she watched the man pulling a piece of glossy paper from the processor. "Oh, what fun! We didn't get to see this when we were in here before."

Somehow, Mrs. Vey was able to tear her out of the darkroom to complete the tour. In another half an hour, Sherri felt that her whole head was buzzing with all the new things she'd seen and heard. She'd never known there was so much detail to the world of providing illustrations and graphic design!

"Sherri, I have just a few things to wrap up and a couple phone calls to make before we're free to go. You just make yourself at home, all right? Nose around if you like."

"Can I go back to the darkroom and watch?" Even to herself, Sherri thought her voice sounded a little breathless.

"Of course. Go right ahead."

It took a moment for her eyes to readjust to the darkness inside. Both men that she'd met earlier were still there.

"Well, hello again." One of them greeted her in a friendly way. "Back for more?"

"Yes. Mrs. Vey said you wouldn't mind if I watched for a while."

"Watch all you want, sister."

She edged closer to the strange-looking machine he was loading negatives into. "What do you call that?" She couldn't help the question.

"This is an enlarger," the man answered. "It's how you decide how much—or what part—of a negative you want in the picture, and also how you control the exposure to the photo paper."

"Exposure?"

"Yeah." The man paused for a moment, squinting down at the image projected below the printer. "You have the same aspects of control when you print a picture as you do when you expose the film in the first place."

"You mean this is like a camera?" Sherri frowned.

"No, not really. It's just transferring the image from the negative to the paper, but it does it by light exposure, the same way you get the image on the negative."

"Oh." Sherri wasn't at all sure she understood him.

"See? Look at the difference." He was twirling a ring on the enlarger back and forth, making the projected image lighter and darker. "Then you can also control a lot by the length of time you expose the paper to the light. Pretty much like the shutter speed on a camera."

Sherri nodded. That much made sense. She quieted down for a while and watched while he adjusted the image within the confines of the little frame that lay on the counter beneath. Then he flicked the light off and twisted a little knob on the nearby timer. Reaching into a drawer below, he pulled out a piece of heavy, glossy paper, flipped up the lid on the frame, inserted the paper, and closed the lid again.

"Presto!" he said, pressing the timer button. The printer light came on, along with the hum of the timer for a few seconds. Then both went off together. "Now you just feed it through the processor. This is an automatic one—real nice. It beats the old way of having to swish it around in trays full of chemicals. This will process from start to finish in about a minute."

"Can you do double exposures with that thing?" Sherri's thoughts were racing in all directions.

"Double exposures?"

"Yes—like two pictures? One cut into another? Whatever it's called. I've seen it done in magazines."

"That's printing—not photography. Ink, not photo paper."

"But can't it be done? Like when they take two pictures of someone and print them together for a graduation picture?"

"Oh, I see. Yeah. Like a vignette or something. Yeah, sure. It's a little harder, but all you have to do is, well, the best way to do it is to get two printers set up and transfer your slate from one enlarger to the other. You have to use a dodger to block the light from the place on the paper where you want the second picture to print—unless you want it to show through real lightly or something. Then you have to do the same with the second, where you don't want it to print over the first."

Sherri squinted at him, trying to follow his train of thought. His answer raised about six new questions in her mind. "What's a dodger?"

"Hey, lady, why don't you just enroll in a photography course?" The second man in the room broke in with a laugh.

"I wish I could." Sherri surprised herself with her own comment. "Maybe someday."

She was sorry when Mrs. Vey entered the darkroom again. "Are you ready to head for home and dinner?"

Home? Somewhere, about ten years ago, Sherri had heard of a place called Rockview Ranch. At the moment she felt like she was on the other side of the world.

"Lynn will be waiting supper on us, Sherri."

Reluctantly she trailed behind the lady to the door. "Thanks, you guys," Sherri called over her shoulder.

"No problem."

The ride to the ranch was a sharp contrast to the earlier drive. Mrs. Vey asked no questions, but Sherri caught her shooting a couple of quick glances in her direction. Sherri had so much food for thought swirling in her head that she could do nothing but lean back against the seat and stare at the passing scenery.

Oh, to have a chance to learn what those people were doing! Would Dad ever okay going into an arts program? Sherri was mentally about two years into the future. But for the first time ever, that future seemed close enough to reach out and touch. What will Dad think? The question wouldn't go away. What will happen if I try it and can't make it? How can I know? She was so preoccupied that she nearly missed pointing out the turnoff to the ranch.

Chapter Nine

Sherri sat on the edge of her bed, slowly flipping through the pages in her small portfolio. She figured it must be her fiftieth trip through, but she still wasn't any more confident about what she was seeing. Even though she had chosen carefully from the stacks and stacks of work she'd done, she felt that it all looked like a sorry excuse for any kind of art. Sketches, lettering, two acrylic paintings, and a fairly large selection of photos. It suddenly looked as though the words "attempt of a child" were stamped across every page.

"Why in the world did I tell her I'd do this?" Sherri groaned aloud. Last night, when Mrs. Vey had asked her to bring some samples of her work by the Krayfor office, Sherri had been ecstatic.

"Sure!" She'd responded after only a moment's hesitation—and the hesitation had been only from surprise, not from lack of desire.

"Good. I'd like to see what direction you're headed in, and if what Lynn has told me is really true." With that, Mrs. Vey had finished the subject, except to tell Sherri to stop by any time this morning.

Lynn had made no comment. Nor did she say anything this morning when she met Sherri in the hallway to the front door.

"I might not be home for lunch." Sherri mumbled, avoiding her stepmother's eyes.

"All right."

Without a backward glance or so much as a goodbye, Sherri hurried out the door. She rummaged in her purse for her set of keys to the station wagon. Halfway down the walk to the garage, Tim burst across her path, apparently shooting up from the ground itself as he always seemed to do. "Where ya going? Can I go too?"

He didn't bother to give her time to answer the first question before asking the second.

"No, Timmy. Not this time."

"Got a date? What ya all dressed up for?" His impish face screwed into a grin. "Come on—let me go!"

"I'm sorry. You can't. I'm going to a business place, Tim. There wouldn't be anything for you to do, anyway."

"Well, can we go for a ride then, when you get back? You haven't taken us all week."

"I know—but it's been busy, okay? We will if I get back in time."

"When are you coming back?"

"I don't know! That's why I said maybe. So don't try and turn it into a promise, okay? And you guys stay away from the barns while I'm gone. I don't care what you think you can get away with, anymore. If I catch you down there, I'll choke the pair of you." She had reached the car door. Opening it, she slid in carefully, trying not to wrinkle her skirt. "Put a strain on yourself now and behave, okay?"

Tim frowned at her, his small face looking unhappy.

"I'll try to get back in time to take a ride. So you and Todd be around here the early part of the afternoon then."

"All right." His frown smoothed out a little as he stepped back and allowed her to close the door.

The drive into town seemed about six times as long as normal. Sherri found the wish growing that she'd either never agreed to do this in the first place, or else that it was already over with. But she couldn't get away from the reality of driving up to level four of the parking garage and crossing the walkway into the Spaldman Building. Her legs felt like shaky rubber as she found her way to the Krayfor lobby.

The room seemed a lot bigger than it had yesterday as she pushed through the glass door and approached the receptionist. Tightening her grip on the portfolio handle, Sherri forced a smile onto her face.

"Hello. Can I help you?" The girl behind the desk seemed friendly enough.

"Yes. I'm here to see Mrs. Vey."

"All right." The receptionist reached for her phone. "Is she expecting you?"

"She told me to stop by sometime this morning."

"And your name?"

"Sherri—James" she added quickly, hoping the gap hadn't been noticeable.

Sherri took relief in the momentary silence while the receptionist dialed a number. At least she knew she didn't have to say anything else for a minute or two.

"Linda, Sherri James is here to see you." The girl's voice was so smooth and professional. Sherri wished that she would let a little more of what she might be thinking show.

A few moments later, Mrs. Vey was coming through the doors behind the desk. "Good morning, Sherri! I'm glad you were able to make it here. Let's go back to my office, shall we?"

Sherri nodded, not able to force words through her dry throat. She followed the lady down the now-familiar short hallway and art department to the quietness of her studio office.

"There, now we can talk in here without being disturbed." Mrs. Vey swung the door shut behind them. "I'm eager to see your things."

"I just brought this." Sherri found her voice somehow, and gestured with the portfolio. "It's not everything, but it's some of the stuff I thought was better than some of the other stuff—you know?"

"Of course. Here, have a seat."

Sherri was surprised that Mrs. Vey took a chair as well, rather than going to her seat behind the desk. She took the portfolio and opened it on her lap.

Sherri's stomach crept into her throat and knotted as the woman paged through, scanning the pieces with total absorption. She watched Mrs. Vey's face, trying to pick up on any change of expression as she went from one piece to another. But the look of concentration never varied.

Sherri was ready to heave a sigh of relief as the last page appeared, but Mrs. Vey started turning backwards, a few pages at a time. More minutes crawled by. In desperation, Sherri started staring at the hands of her wristwatch instead. Ten minutes. Fifteen.

"Tell me about these." Mrs. Vey's question nearly made Sherri leap from her seat.

"What—oh those pictures?" Sherri leaned forward to see exactly what was on the page.

"Yes."

"They're, ah—well, I took them last summer at Pine Bench. It's part of our ranch, but it's way up in the high country."

"Pine Bench?"

"Yeah—yes. See, there and there, and up here." Sherri leaned forward to point at several of the photos. "There's a high strip of land—a bench—that runs around the north rim of the valley. It's mostly covered with jackpine. That's where it gets its name."

"It looks like a lovely place."

"Oh, it is! It's one of the prettiest places on our ranch." Sherri warmed to her subject a little. "Those pictures don't even begin to tell you, but there's one thing," she leaned forward again and pointed to another picture. "Right there. You can hardly see them, but those are wild horses."

"Really?" Mrs. Vey took a closer look.

"Um-hmm. Pine Bench is right on the northeast corner of our place. Beyond our line is a federal reserve. The horses are over there, mostly, but they come up to our place a lot. If it weren't for the reserve property, Dad would have busted their bunch up a long time ago. But he can't chase them while they are on federal property."

A smile touched Mrs. Vey's mouth. "Your dad doesn't care much for wild horses?"

"They're pests on a ranch. They eat valuable feed and lots of times a stud will make off with ranch mares. Plus, most wild horses are just scrub. Junk. They inbreed a lot, and they don't get all the food they need while they're growing. They're not usually worth a whole lot."

Sherri sat back in her chair and tried to halt her flow of chatter; but since Mrs. Vey seemed interested, she found herself going on. "That bunch up there is a little different. The stallion is—was—a ranch stallion from a place on the far side of the reserve. He carries a brand, but I bet he hasn't seen the inside of a corral in fifteen or twenty years. He broke away as a two-year-old and has been loose ever since. He has good bloodlines, I guess, and has made a real career of stealing mares from ranches all over, so there're some beautiful horses in that herd. I'd love to get some good pictures of them someday, but it's really hard to get close enough."

"The horses are pretty spooky, then?"

"Spooky isn't the word. If that stallion—Pharitell is his name—gets any idea that you're within twenty miles, the whole bunch is gone in a blink."

Mrs. Vey looked back at pictures. The silence grew again, but somehow, Sherri didn't feel quite as uncomfortable.

"Sherri." Mrs. Vey stood up and closed the portfolio, handing it back to her. "I'm sure you're wondering what this is all about."

Sherri nodded, not trusting her voice.

"I'll be completely up front with you. I asked you over here yesterday and today because I am scouting for a student helper. I have had one—different ones, of course—for the last ten or fifteen years. Michelle, my most recent, graduated this spring—she went to Centerville Academy. I haven't been satisfied with several other possibilities that I've looked into."

Sherri gripped the handle of the portfolio, not daring to believe what was coming to her mind.

"It wasn't until day before yesterday that Lynn called me. She knew of Michelle, also, and was wondering if I was looking for a replacement for her. She suggested that I might be interested in you. I was interested, of course, but not until I had a chance to talk to you and see for myself what your abilities are."

Mrs. Vey finally took her seat behind the desk. "So it was no chance that I came to the dentist's office yesterday."

Sherri still said nothing. Day before yesterday, she thought. That was the day Lynn saw the sketch. She shook that from her mind for a moment and wondered if Mrs. Vey could possibly mean it.

"Sherri, do you understand what I'm saying?" Mrs. Vey said with a smile.

"I'm not sure."

The smile grew wider. "I like what I've seen. You have potential. A good deal of it. If you don't mind being a Girl Friday for a lot of my projects, I'd like you to think about working here for me—it would be a part-time job. Both this summer and during the school year."

"Doing what?" Sherri's voice turned into a croak. In a panic she thought, how can I do anything like what she'd expect?

"You'd do a lot of things: paste-up work on mechanicals, some typesetting, as you're able to learn to use the equipment, some lab work in the darkroom, and, possibly, some design work, depending on how well you progress."

Mrs. Vey seemed to be waiting for a comment.

"I don't even know what most of the things are that you just mentioned." Sherri felt she had to be honest.

"You could learn. They're just terms—terms for things that I can already see you have aptitude for. There's a lot you'd have to learn, but that's always part of taking a new job. Are you interested?"

"Yes!" The single word flew out, but then Sherri hesitated. "But I'm not sure how this is going to go over at home."

"Well, you'll just have to go home and see, then."

"Do you really think I can do what you want me to do?"

"I wouldn't have asked you if I didn't. Now, Sherri, this isn't a high-paying job, and there will be a lot of repetitious things that you might find boring. But there is one advantage for you—besides a lot of experience that you're not going to gain at your high school. As an employee here, you would have access to using the facilities and equipment for your own personal or freelance work—such as the cameras and darkroom that you arc so fascinatcd with." Mrs. Vcy smilcd at her thunderstruck expression.

"As for your schedule, for this summer, it would be three days a week—Monday through Wednesday are the days that I do most of my in-office work and would need you here. During the school year, it would be most days after school for two or three hours, but you would have your weekends free, I promise."

"I'm not sure what Dad's going to say. There are a lot of things I'm supposed to do after school at home."

"Well, like I said, you'll have to clear this with him. But if you decide you want the job, you may consider it yours."

"Dad's gone for a few days."

"Yes, I know. That's all right. You just give me a call here at this number when you make up your mind." Mrs. Vey handed Sherri a business card.

Sherri looked at it, fingering the raised letters of the Krayfor Agency logo and Mrs. Vey's name. Was this really happening to her, she wondered.

"Mrs. Vey?"

"Yes?"

"Did Lynn talk you into this?"

A momentary silence filled the room to the bursting point.

"Sherri, I've told you the truth, dear. Lynn brought you to my attention, but the decision is mine alone. I see some potential in your work, particularly your photography and graphics. I like to give aspiring young artists any boost I can. This is one way I can do it and meet a need of my own at the same time. Understand?"

Sherri looked up into the dark eyes. They were gazing back with frank honesty that she could not doubt.

"Yes, ma'am."

"Very well." Mrs. Vey's expression softened. "I've enjoyed talking to you. You can see yourself out—and give me a call as soon as you know your decision."

"Thank you!" Sherri broke into a radiant smile as the reality of the situation began to sink in. All the way to the car, she hardly even felt the ground beneath her feet.

Chapter Ten

Sherri had no idea how to broach the subject of the job—whether to even bring it up at all. She wondered whether it might be better to wait until her father got home. But at the same time, she had a feeling that his reaction wasn't going to be all that positive. She could hear the answer already. "Sherri, I can't be running in and out of town all the time to get you. And there're things here that you need to be doing."

You'll never have another chance like this. It could make all the difference in the world, Sherri told herself fiercely. Get some backbone and figure out what you're going to say.

Just the same, she felt her courage shriveling already. How many times had she heard him say it—"Honey, you spend too much time thinking about frivolous things. Too much dreaming. You need to use your head for practicality a little more."

If he'd ever just listen to me, Sherri thought. But she knew that wasn't quite fair. Maybe if she could just get up the nerve to talk to him a little more about it! But self-rebuke wasn't making her feel any better—nor did it give her a better idea about what she was supposed to do.

Reaching home, Sherri slipped in the back door and changed her clothes without letting Lynn know she was back.

Letting herself out again with equal stealth, she scouted around till she found Timmy and Todd. It wasn't difficult. Once she was far enough from the house so that she wouldn't automatically be heard, all she had to do was whistle for Dash. The big shepherd was like a homing beacon for the kids, though his dignity was greatly pained these last few days by the gamboling puppy. It had been a long time since she'd taken the boys out on a good long ride. So this time she set a brisk pace, meaning to take them all the way to Crest Spring. That meant a steep climb and a total distance covered of about seven miles.

Actually, both boys were getting to be pretty good little riders. With specific permission, they were allowed to ride in the empty corrals when someone was around to keep an eye on them. Otherwise, the corral areas were strictly off-limits for a few more years. But they did spend a lot of time trying to copy their father's riding, and several times Sherri had seen them whacking a patient cow horse in the ears with a lariat, trying to figure out how to throw the rope. But their day would come. Already Sherri was beginning to see traces of Shane's and Terry's competence in their manner.

The boys' fast-developing image of themselves as cow-hands kept them from complaining about the fast pace, but by the time they returned to the barn, she knew they were aching to get out of their saddles. Sherri was hot and uncomfortable herself, and she had been glad for the distraction of their chatter during the ride. It kept her mind off the impending decision. At least she had thought it was going to be a decision. As it turned out, the matter was taken off her hands.

Lynn or no Lynn, Sherri knew that she had to have a drink or keel over. So she came in through the kitchen door this time. Crossing to the sink first, she rinsed her hands and splashed some water on her face. Pulling the hand towel down to dry herself with, she leaned limply over the sink, her elbows on the edge of the counter.

"Tired?" Lynn's bright voice came from the dining room door.

"It's hot." Sherri didn't really turn around until she'd hung up the towel. Even then, she went straight for the refrigerator and began rummaging for a Coke. The debate was still raging in her mind when Lynn spoke again.

"Well." There was a note of amusement in the cool voice. "Did she offer you the job?"

"Did she—what?" Sherri almost choked on her first swallow.

"Did she offer you the job?"

Sherri thought furiously for a moment. Of course, you fool, she told herself with annoyance. Mrs. Vey told you this was her idea in the first place! She took another long swallow of the Coke before she finally answered. "Yes." She couldn't bring herself to say more.

At that Lynn crossed the room and seated herself on a counter stool. She inspected Sherri closely. "What did you tell her?"

"I told her I didn't know if I could." Sherri slammed the refrigerator door shut, avoiding her stepmother's eyes.

"Why?"

"Cause I figure Dad's going to tell me to forget it."

"Why?"

"Because!" Sherri felt her irritation rising. "Because— because that's just the way it is."

"Don't you think he'd like what you'd be doing?"

"It's not that. He just doesn't think it's any big deal. Besides, he never let Terry or Shane get jobs. Not even Terry with his computers. The ranch is supposed to be a 'family business.' "

"Do you feel that way? That it's 'no big deal,' I mean."

"No!"

There was a long silence. Sherri just leaned back against the refrigerator door and stared at the floor.

"Sherri, what do you want to do about college?"

"I'm not sure." Sherri squeezed a dent in her can.

"I thought that perhaps you might be interested in a degree in some field of art."

Another long pause. Sherri had to risk a glance up at Lynn before answering. The woman's eyes were frank and sympathetic—if a little speculative.

"I don't know if I could. And, again, I don't know what Dad would say."

"Have you ever talked to him about it?"

"Not really. I guess I just frustrate him, gabbing about it when there's so much else going on. And I don't like to bring it up because—well— " Sherri stopped herself abruptly, realizing that she seemed to be talking awfully freely about things that she never talked about to anyone—let alone to Lynn.

"Sherri." Lynn took a deep breath and released it in a sigh before continuing. "Some art programs at the college level are pretty tough. You have a lot of ability, I think, but the training that this job would give you would make things a lot easier later."

"I know that!" Sherri felt a little exasperated. She couldn't really see where all this was leading. "But three days a week— and every night after school! That's like until five or five-thirty. Dad would flip. It's barely enough time to get home before dinner. There's too much going on here—stuff that I have to be here for."

"Even now?"

Sherri felt a flush rising in her face. Lynn didn't need to explain. "I think so, yes. At least I figure he'll think so."

"Sherri, I'm not trying to be difficult, but just supposing that your dad was agreeable, what other problems would there be?"

"Well." Sherri thought for a moment. "Even if he thought it was okay, I know he couldn't ever take the time to come after me—and you'd be busy, too, at that time of day. Terry will be tied up with classes, and Shane gone altogether."

"I thought perhaps you could use my car."

Sherri's head jerked up. Was she hearing right? There wasn't anybody else here to impress, so Lynn must be sincere. The quiet seemed to beat against Sherri's temples in little waves. She studied the ring on the top of her Coke can.

"I guess, well, I don't know . . . why not? I mean. . . ." Sherri couldn't seem to find her sense of logical speech patterns. She walked to the screen door and stared out across the patio, taking a long drink. The silence continued its pulsing, growing thicker by the moment.

"It would take a miracle. . . ." Sherri remembered her own words, but she'd hardly been thinking on such a tremendous scale! *"Call unto me, and I will answer thee, and shew thee great and mighty things, which thou knowest not."* The old Sunday school memory verses spoke up on their own.

Sherri heard the faint scream of an eagle as he soared over the slopes to the north. Looking up, she scanned the sky until she saw the bird dive toward the horizon. Say something! she ordered herself. Say anything! Make something up!

Like what, though? Like "Oh, Lynn, I changed my mind. I'm so glad you're here?" Sherri wondered whether that's what the woman was waiting to hear. Well, she didn't intend to lie.

You could at least say *thank you,* her conscience reprimanded her.

She swallowed several times. Then all at once, she turned quickly around. "Lynn, I think—" But she stopped in surprise. The stool was empty and Lynn was gone.

Chapter Eleven

The herd's return caught everyone by surprise. They were expected, but not till late in the day. Sherri was sitting on the back patio with her sketch pad, working on a close-up sketch of Dash's head. He was lying stretched full-length before her, twitching his nose and ears occasionally at the flies.

She probably wouldn't have noticed at all, except that Dash suddenly raised his head and looked inquisitively toward the north pasture. A whine quivered through his throat. As a natural reflex, Sherri looked up. The herd was breaking over the ridge by the Crest Spring trail.

"Whoops!" She leaped to her feet and made for the kitchen door. She nearly bowled Lynn over as she passed through the hallway on the run for her bedroom. "They're here!" She didn't break stride, but raced into her room, kicked off her loafers, and pulled on her boots.

"I thought they wouldn't be in till late today." Lynn had followed her.

"Me too. But they're here. You can bank on that." As she spoke, Sherri heard Dandy's shrill whistle from the barn. It came again as she made a fast grab for a hair elastic. Bundling her blonde mass into a ponytail, she made for the door.

"What's the rush?" Lynn seemed a little taken aback by her scurrying.

"They'll need to run the herd into separate pens. It's easier if you can do it right away as they come in. But the horses are still in the holding pen. We'll have to get them out and be ready at this end before they get across the pasture." Sherri's voice was rising as she took off down the path at a run. She knew she probably wasn't making much sense to Lynn. "Come and watch if you want!" she called back.

As she neared the barn, she heard Dandy's whistles and whoops to the horses. She knew he was hurrying to get them out of the center pen. The herd, twenty strong, came thundering toward the entrance to the alleyway. Sherri grabbed a lariat from the fence post, dove through the rails, and swung the gate open to the chute into the barn. Taffy was right at the front of the group.

"Whoa! Hey!" she shouted, stepping to the left of the mare and shooing her in as they poured past. Another young gelding attempted to follow her, but Sherri expertly swung the gate shut, cutting him off.

"Get on, now!" She waved the rest of them on down to the smaller pen toward the back of the barn. As the last one went by, she slammed the entry gate and raced back to the barn.

Taffy was wandering aimlessly through the main aisle of the barn, snuffling for any misplaced grain. Sherri yanked her gear out of the tack room, grabbed a container of oats, and rattled it. Taffy approached with pointed interest. Sherri draped the bridle over her neck and let her eat while she made short work of cinching up her saddle. "Okay, mare, that's enough." She pulled Taffy's head back and slipped the bridle on.

Tossing the container back into the bin, Sherri led Taffy outside. Dandy was just tightening up the girth on his bay.

"Everything ready?" she asked.

"Yeah. Wish they'd stick to their dumb schedule. Got those horses so riled, it'll take 'em a week to settle down. There's young stock in there that don't need that kind of stuff, an—"

Sherri grinned and pretty much quit listening. Dandy felt he had to keep up his reputation of grumpiness. Her grin disappeared as she turned around. Todd and Timmy were rounding the corner from the front of the barn. "What are you guys doing down here?" Sherri started to reprimand them, but then Lynn came around right behind them. "Oh. Okay." But long experience made her give them the reminder anyway. "You boys stay out of the chutes, out of the pens, and off the rails, got it?"

Two heads nodded.

"In fact, the auction deck is probably the best place for you. If you don't mind, Lynn."

"Not at all. Come on, guys. Let's go up where we can see the action." Lynn led them up the stairs that went to the elevated announcer's box attached to the side of the barn.

Sherri swung up onto Taffy and headed her toward the far end of the corrals. She walked her back and forth to loosen her muscles, Dandy doing the same with his mount, as they waited for the herd to reach them. They watched, able to see that the cattle were restless and upset. As they approached, Shane rode up hard on one flank and Luke on the opposite. Everybody went into action like a well-rehearsed team.

All cattle were driven into the chute toward the main pen. Then the stock that was already marked with green spray went into one pen for sale. All young stock, from the yearlings to the spring-borns, had to be separated, either for medical treatment, vaccinations, branding, or some such thing—just as they had done with the outbound herd a few days ago. It was a hot, dirty, exhausting process. The choking dust was constantly swirling up to cake in Sherri's eyes and cover her mouth and throat with grit. The cattle were rambunctious, aggressive, and hard to control. More than once an angry cow slammed into Sherri's leg, making her feel as though it were breaking the bone. She had always hated this part of the drive, but it was an inescapable fact of life.

The man-against-cow struggle went on throughout the day, with only a quick break for lunch. Once everything was separated into the proper pen, the vaccinations, testings, and brandings had to be carried out. They would barely get a start today, Sherri realized, as the late afternoon sunbeams slanted through the dust, making grimy sparkles among the herd.

But it was nearly dark before her father called a halt. "Great," he praised his crew. "We'll have the yearlings to finish in the morning, and then we can start the dipping."

A round chorus of groans went up at this announcement.

"What's 'dipping'?" Lynn asked a little while later at the supper table. She seemed to be about the only person besides the youngest boys who had any desire to talk. The rest of the family was falling on the food as though they hadn't seen it for months.

"It's torture." Kyle spoke up dryly. "Torture to the muscles, mind, and nose."

"What?" Lynn's amused smile grew.

"It's a grim subject for the table, honey." Sherri's father smiled as he watched the faces that everyone made. "It's a process of swimming the herd, a few at a time, through a tank of disinfectant. Lots of work. And lots of mess. The cattle hate it worse than we do."

"How often do you have to do this?" Lynn seemed oddly curious.

"Once or twice a year. It depends." Shane answered. "But that's once or twice too often. Bluhh!"

"Hmm." Lynn finally let the conversation go. Not even Sherri caught the glint in her eye as she returned her attention to her dinner.

Sherri crawled out of bed the next morning in the predawn blackness. She wasn't looking forward to the upcoming day, but maybe, she thought, if things really went well, her dad would be in a good enough mood tonight for her to approach about the job idea.

She was still turning this idea over in her mind at the breakfast table when Terry brought up an unpopular subject. "Hey, Sherri." He was half-teasing, half-serious. "This time you're going to do your share at the far end. I am not standing there all day, getting that junk shaken and dripped all over me."

Sherri stuck out her tongue at him. Everybody hated to be at the end where the cattle came out of the dip, for the very reasons he'd just stated. But before she could think of a good retort, Lynn spoke up in a very casual tone.

"I think that you guys are going to have to take your turns without Sherri today. I'm going to be needing her here."

All the way around the table, forkfuls of scrambled eggs and sausage halted. Sherri was the first to recover. She took a big bite, put her fork down, and stared at her stepmother.

Even her father stared blankly at his wife. Sherri waited for him to laugh at the joke, but he didn't. Lynn met his gaze evenly, with a sweet and slightly bland smile. Some unspoken communication seemed to pass between them, for he abruptly cleared his throat and took another bite. "Right. Well, fine. If you need her here, that's fine."

"You've gotta be kidding!" Terry's exclamation seemed to echo the feeling of the rest.

"Of course not." Lynn's voice was still unruffled. "I'm sure you guys can struggle along without one lone little female, can't you?"

"She's better than that!" Kyle spoke up in automatic defense.

"Nevertheless." Lynn's tone was firm.

"Well, gang, let's get going, hey?" Sherri's dad seemed anxious to end the discussion, if it could be called that. She got the distinct feeling that something was making him uncomfortable. He didn't meet her eyes or make another comment as the guys cleared out in a shuffle of general grumbling.

Sherri sat still, breakfast forgotten. She stared at Lynn in silence until she heard the door bang behind her brothers. Then she could contain herself no longer. What was she in for today? Did she have any choice in whatever the matter was?

"What. . . . " But Sherri's voice wandered away after the one syllable. She couldn't even think of the words for her question.

Lynn's smile grew broader as she stood up and began pulling plates toward her. Picking up silverware in a businesslike manner, she spoke matter-of-factly. "There's a mall over near Centerville that I've heard has the best shopping in the area. As soon as we get these dishes cleared off, I need you to act as navigator to get me over there."

"Forest Mall? Why? I mean why today?" Sherri was beginning to feel really out of touch.

"It beats dipping cattle, doesn't it?"

Sherri hesitated only a moment. "Just about anything does."

"Well, then." Lynn seemed to be putting a finishing touch on a point that Sherri hadn't quite gotten yet. Lynn's smile grew amused as she picked up a stack of dishes. Instead of moving toward the kitchen with them, she stood still, facing her stepdaughter. "Sherri, it all comes in the same package. You are not a ranch hand."

Comprehension broke over Sherri in a rush, but she still wasn't sure what to think. She quickly decided to borrow a phrase from her dad. "Right," she said, with a lot more certainty than she felt. She jumped to her feet and began gathering dishes, stopping only for a moment to listen to Lynn's light humming from the kitchen.

They waited until Mrs. Andersen arrived. Todd and Tim were still asleep when they left. "I'll look out for them. You two run along." Sherri could tell that Mrs. Andersen was pleased to see her going somewhere with Lynn.

On the long drive to Centerville, Lynn kept up a running flow of chatter. She talked about various department stores, things she needed to look for in summer wear for herself and the rest of the family, and asked Sherri's advice on several things that she might need now that she was living on a ranch. Sherri answered her as readily as she was able but had the distinct feeling that she was two people. One person was the one sitting in the little red car chatting away with her stepmother, and the other was someone else who sat nearby, wondering if she was losing her mind. Twenty-four hours ago, Sherri hadn't had a single word to say to this woman—and she would have rather dipped cattle until Christmas than go anywhere with her. What was going on? Was it all just because of this business about the job?

They arrived at Forest Mall as the stores were opening. Sherri quickly realized that this was not going to be like any trip she'd ever taken with other members of her family. They took their time, wandering in and out of stores, investigating whatever caught their fancy. No one fussed at her to hurry up, and no one made her go through sport shops. Lynn didn't so much as comment when Sherri got stalled for forty-five minutes in the camera shop, poring over sales literature and the display items.

Lynn purchased a few items: a Western-style hat for herself, at Sherri's recommendation, and some jeans for Todd and Tim. She picked out some boots for herself, too, but decided to wait on buying them until right before they left so she wouldn't have to lug them around.

It was nearly noon when Lynn stopped suddenly as they passed the window of a small boutique. "Oh, Sherri, look at that! Isn't it beautiful?" Lynn gestured at the dress on a mannequin in the window.

"It's nice," Sherri agreed. Her gaze ran over the jade-colored material, appreciating the tailored look of the dress. It had three-quarter-length sleeves, a high collar that was open in the front, a fitted waist, and a full skirt.

"Let's go have a look." Lynn was through the door in an instant, leaving Sherri nothing to do but follow. They found the dress on display before a salesclerk had a chance to approach them.

Lynn swept the dress off the rack and held it up against Sherri. "Oh, how perfect with your coloring! Look!" Lynn swiveled her around to the mirror on the wall.

Sherri gave a nearly visible start as she saw the green in her eyes leap out to match the shade of the material. She almost didn't hear the clerk.

"May I help you?"

"Yes," Lynn answered. "She'd like to try this on. What size, Sherri?"

"What?" Sherri faced her stepmother again with a puzzled frown. "Why?"

"It's a beautiful color for you! Just try it on. What size do you usually wear?"

"Seven," Sherri stammered. "But—"

"Nonsense. Shoo in there now. I want to see that dress on you. Where's your sense of adventure?"

Sherri quickly found herself in the dressing room, pulling the green dress over her head and struggling with the fastenings. She had barely finished when Lynn brushed through the curtain behind her.

"Oh, Sherri, honey, look at you!"

Sherri looked, once again feeling a mild sense of shock. There was nothing extravagant about the dress. Its lines and styling were clean to the point of simplicity, but she had never felt so well matched in her life as she stared at her reflection. She took a deep breath as though she wanted to say something, but no words came. Lynn must have seen the question in her eyes, for she dropped her packages on the chair and came forward.

"It's mostly in the coloring, Sherri. You're a blonde with a lot more golden tone in your skin than I have. Things with a base color like brown, yellow, orange, or whatever will look a lot better on you than clear, bluish colors, or ones with a base of pure white. See, there's a lot of yellow in the green here."

Sherri nodded. Her artistic eye could see that what Lynn was saying was true. But somehow she'd never thought of trying to match colors to herself as she would a painting to a frame.

"A gold necklace, probably." Lynn was running on ahead of Sherri's thoughts. "Do you have a short one?"

"Um-hmm." Sherri was beginning to feel a little overwhelmed.

"Good, and let's see. What about shoes? Do you have black? Or would that even be best? It's a fall dress—you won't be wearing it for a while yet."

Neither of them had heard the saleslady approach. "We carry a shoe dyed to match that dress." The lady spoke pleasantly.

A whirl of events followed, and Sherri presently found herself outside the shop with a package tucked under her arm.

"Dad's going to have a fit." That was all Sherri could think of to say.

"I don't think so." Lynn smiled. "Or I wouldn't have bought it for you."

"I just don't know." Sherri was still a little dubious. "I've never. . . ." Her voice trailed off.

"I know you haven't." Lynn's expression was suddenly serious. "But that doesn't mean you can't ever, does it?"

Sherri looked at her sharply. Her mind brought up a swift picture of Kathleen as she'd seen her that first night, sitting in the chair by the fireplace. Scarcely conscious of what she did, Sherri took a tighter grip on the package.

Chapter Twelve

Dinner that night seemed strange to Sherri. The guys were tired. That was to be expected. Rarely after a day of dipping did anyone have much to say at the table. But tonight it seemed that the silence was extra thick. Once or twice, Sherri even caught Kyle giving her a reproachful glance.

The only topic of general interest was the upcoming horse auction in town the next Saturday. Then it was only a reminder from their father that those who wanted to go should make sure that their work was done by 9:00 A.M., because he wanted to be there when the exhibits opened up.

"Are we going on a buying trip?" Lynn was curious.

Sherri realized that no one had thought to explain to her about Rockview's "horse trading" business.

"Yes," Sherri answered, when no one else seemed about to. "Once or twice a year, we go and get a bunch of new stock—greenbrokes and unbroken horses. Three- and four-year-olds, mostly. We keep them here through the year and train them as we have time. Their resale value is a lot higher than what we buy them for."

"Do you usually sell them all?"

"Oh, sure. Plus we have a bunch of young ones that are foaled here on the ranch. We'd sell more if we had the time to train more. Word gets around that people can usually pick up a good stock horse here."

"Speaking of which, Sherri," her father perked up for a moment, "Calvin Peller told me in town the other day that he's decided to take Tramp. You give him a call in the morning and set up a time to take that gelding over to him."

"Yes, sir."

"Is that one of the ones you're talking about?" Lynn asked.

"Um-hmm. Tramp is the bay that I ride sometimes. He's one of the last of the bunch we bought last fall."

Conversation dwindled after that. When the meal was over, her father read from Philippians. Sherri lost the train of thought after a few verses because her mind got stuck on one particular part: *Being confident of this very thing, that he which hath begun a good work in you will perform it until the day of Jesus Christ.*

Sherri was still mulling that over as she finished the dishes with the help of Todd and Tim. Never in her life had she been given so much food for thought in such a short time. Was it the Lord who was changing things so rapidly in her life? For years Sherri had heard pastors, teachers, and her father talk about how the Lord "led" them to do certain things. Though she believed what they said, Sherri had to admit that her own experience with the concept was pretty short. It had never seemed before like she'd had many options about what she was or was not going to do.

But was this what people meant? Was this constant unrest of her conscience and the thoughts that kept springing up of their own accord actually the Lord trying to tell her something? She flicked off the light over the sink and looped the dishtowel over its hook. What else could account for the strange whirl of recent events? "I'm listening, Lord," she said silently. "Or at least I'm trying to. I'm just really confused."

But it wasn't until the next day that Sherri's mental turmoil reached its height. She had enlisted Kyle's help to hook up the small, two-horse trailer to the ranch truck. Mr. Peller had said that he'd be glad to have the horse right away. The dipping had to be finished, but Sherri needed help to move the horse.

Now, with the trailer hooked up and the lights checked out, Sherri was leading Tramp out to put him in. She was nearly to the trailer when her father's voice halted her.

"Sherri?"

"Sir?"

"Could I see you for a moment?" He spoke from the door of the barn.

"Yes, sir."

Kyle stepped forward and took Tramp.

"Wait a minute. Don't put him in till I'm ready. He might not like having to stand. I don't think he's been trailered by himself before."

"Okay." Kyle moved the bay to the side of the driveway and let him munch on the short grass. Sherri quickly retraced her steps and discovered her father sitting on a bale of hay in front of the tack room.

"Have a seat."

Sherri complied by propping herself against the feed bin. She didn't say anything but waited for her father to speak. She had to wait a few moments though. And even then she thought, as she had on several occasions recently, her dad seemed uncomfortable.

"Sherri, I, ah. I know you didn't intend to bring this up yet. But Lynn told me about it last night." He paused. "The job, I mean."

"Oh." Sherri looked down, her heart leaping into her throat. Great. Resentment flared up all over again. Did that woman always have to butt in? This wasn't the way Sherri had planned things at all. She didn't know yet what she intended to say, or how she intended to convince him to let her try.

"I take it you want to do this?"

She nodded carefully.

"Tell me about it." He stretched his feet forward and leaned back against the wall.

Whatever Sherri had expected, that wasn't it. "Well . . ." She hesitated. "I'd be working as an assistant to Mrs. Vey, who is their Art Director. I guess I'd be doing a lot of different things. A lot of paste-up work—putting together the mechanicals that they use to print things from. Photocopying things according to different dimensions. Depending on how good I get, she said I might be able to do some darkroom work with the cameras and printing and stuff like that. Maybe eventually I'd even be able to do some design on little projects. It all depends."

Excitement crept into her voice as she spoke. "I'll be able to watch all the different things they do. Graphics, illustrations, computer graphics, slide shows—everything. They're the best agency anywhere near here. Everybody says so. Dad, it's not even so much what I could do there as it is what I'd have the chance to be around."

She stopped, hearing in her own voice that she was beginning to sound overanxious. But to her surprise, her father just continued to watch her, nodding. "Go on," he finally said.

"There's just so much I could learn." Sherri looked away again, biting her lip. As soon as she got to thinking about his reaction instead of what she was saying, she lost her nerve. Why couldn't he just say yes or no and get it over with?

"You know I never let the boys work in town."

I should have been a prophet, Sherri told herself. Yes, she knew the whole theory. The ranch was a family project. Her dad was willing enough to finance such things as hobbies and college tuition, as long as everyone did his share at Rockview. It was fair enough, really, but it didn't boost her spirits at the moment.

"But there's no graphic arts on the ranch, I realize. And I want to be fair about what I told you last week. Things are a little different for you than for your brothers. It's just been easy for me to forget about that." He pulled a green piece of hay out of the bale on which he sat and chewed on it thoughtfully. "Why do you want to learn about this kind of thing, Sherri?" He was studying her face with an intentness that made her want to squirm.

She looked at him in surprise, not sure whether his question was sincere. Shouldn't the answer be obvious?

"Is that what you want to do? Permanently, I mean." He must have gotten tired of waiting for an answer.

Sherri nodded, gripping the edges of the feed bin so hard that her knuckles showed white.

A long silence followed before he spoke again. "Why haven't you ever told me this before?"

Sherri shrugged. She looked away from him, out the barn door to the driveway. Somehow, her willingness to talk openly was fast evaporating. She heard his heavy sigh as he shifted position on the bale of hay.

"Lynn tells me that you have a lot of talent."

Sherri still didn't answer. What's a person supposed to say to that, she wondered. When her father spoke again, his voice sounded faraway, almost as though he were speaking to himself instead of to her.

"You get more like your mother every day."

Sherri risked a swift glance at him, but he wasn't even looking her. His gaze was drifting vacantly across the barn, so she looked away again, quickly, before their eyes could cross paths.

"All right." The statement was so matter-of-fact that Sherri didn't even realize what he was saying.

"All right, what?" she said. Her voice betrayed the tension inside.

"All right. Do it."

It was a good thing she'd been sitting down. She faced her father with a wide-eyed stare. "Really?"

"Yes, really. With a couple conditions."

"What?"

"What are your plans for the money?"

"Ten per cent tithe, half to college savings, and I buy my own clothes and gas," Sherri rattled off. That question, at least, she had anticipated. She saw her father smother a smile.

"Okay. But one other thing."

"Sir?"

"I want to see the portfolio that you showed to Mrs. Vey. Tonight, if possible."

With a quick nod to hide a surge of pleasure, Sherri yanked her scattered thoughts together in a hurry and rushed to the truck. She repeated the whole conversation to Kyle on the way to Pellers. His reaction was one of bewilderment and a touch of disgust. "You never showed me any portfolio, either."

"I didn't think you'd want to see it." Truthfully, she'd been afraid he wouldn't think her work was any good. There was one thing guaranteed about junior-high brothers: honesty.

"Why do you want to do that stuff, Sherri? It sounds awful boring to me."

"I love it. It's fun. Fascinating. Especially the photography. Kyle! I can use all their equipment—and do my own developing and printing. At wholesale prices for supplies, even. I'd pay them to let me work there, if I could."

Kyle snorted. "I wouldn't pay anybody to let me work for them. I think you're a brick or two short of a load."

Sherri rolled her window down and propped her elbow on the opening. At the moment she didn't care what anyone thought. Her mind was spinning on to the wonderful possibilities of the weeks ahead.

They made the delivery to the Pellers without undue excitement. Mr. Peller was curious about whether or not they had any more stock for sale. "No," Sherri told him. "We'll probably pick up some more at the auction this weekend, but spring is busy for us, and we haven't had time to keep much of a line going. There's a couple that are halfway along, but it'll be a month or two before Dad will consider selling."

"Have you seen anything of the auction stock yet?" Mr. Peller asked.

"No, sir. We won't until Saturday morning. We generally go early, though. Dad likes to look around."

They did go early, too. It turned out to be an all-family outing. Sherri was still full of thoughts about her job as they piled into the station wagon for the trip to town. Mrs. Vey had seemed pleased when Sherri called to accept the job. She was to start a week from Monday, since Mrs. Vey would be out of town this next week. How fast things can change, Sherri thought, as she watched Terry carefully driving the truck behind them.

"Oh, Lord," her silent prayer was impulsive. "Help me not to be so quick to get frustrated with circumstances. I'm beginning to see that if I can just wait to see how it will all turn out. . . . " Sherri's thoughts raced ahead to the week after next. She couldn't decide whether her excitment or nervousness was greater.

They were some of the first people to arrive at the display barns. Most of the horses being offered for sale were in box stalls, with the top halves of the doors open for viewing. A few of the more ambitious sellers had their horses out, walking them around, riding them in the ring, or working them on lunge lines.

For a couple of hours, the James entourage walked around the barns looking for prospects while Sherri's dad made notes on his auction list.

"Hey, Dad! Look at that!" Sherri was careful to keep her voice low. It never did any good to display a big interest in a particular horse.

"What? Oh." He followed her gaze to a liver-colored gelding being led across the aisle in the next barn.

"Hello!" Shane whistled softly. "He's a good-looker!"

Casually they sauntered toward his stall. Sherri craned her neck to see around her father and brothers. The gelding was medium height, perhaps fifteen-two. His color was solid liver chestnut from the tip of his ears to the top of his hooves;

mane and tail were the same hue. Sherri couldn't see a white hair anywhere. She looked him over with a practiced eye: large, muscled hindquarters, short body, sloping shoulders, well-proportioned legs and feet. His head was classically quarter horse—straight line from forehead to nose, wide forehead, and small ears.

No one said anything, but Sherri saw her father glance at the horse's number and mark his pad. She had a feeling that, short of an outrageous asking price, the gelding would be going home with them.

When the afternoon bidding started, her dad had twenty-eight horses marked on his sale list as worthwhile prospects. When the bidding concluded, seven of those prospects were loaded onto the Rockview van for a careful drive home.

Sherri sat in the station wagon and watched the liver gelding, named Impressive Cedar, in the back of the trailer. She wondered whether she'd get a chance to get in on his training. He sure was a beauty. But even with such a tempting horse before her eyes, Sherri found that her thoughts would not stay away from the upcoming first day of her new job. With a small jolt, she realized that she almost didn't care whether her father said someone else could break the gelding.

Chapter Thirteen

It was wry justice, Sherri thought as she sat in Lynn's car and stared toward the house. Today of all days. She knew it had been too perfect. Sitting in the curve of the driveway was a small blue car that she recognized as Kathleen's.

"There goes the summer," she said aloud. She scraped up her purse and stepped out of the car. All she wanted right now was to sit down somewhere and revel in what she was sure had been the most interesting day of her life.

She was now an official member of the Krayfor staff, albeit a part-time, student member. Today, on her first day, Mrs. Vey had assigned her to another young girl, Francine, to be shown the basics of "paste-up." Paste-up was the stage of actually arranging the pieces of print and artwork on a stiff piece of pasteboard—a "mechanical," as they called it— so that it could be sent to the camera, and film and plates could be made for printing.

It was exacting work, requiring a lot of care and concentration. Things had to be straight, clean, square, and exactly according to the designer's specifications, to the fraction of an inch, or "point" as they called it. Sherri had started learning a whole new system of measurement: points, picas, leading, kerning—her mind was swamped with new information. But she'd never been more willing to apply herself. She'd spent most of her day working on paste-up for a brochure. Sherri glowed in spite of her cramped neck and shoulders when her finished product brought praise from Mrs. Vey.

For the remainder of the afternoon, Mrs. Vey had turned her over to the darkroom supervisor, who began to teach her the involved processes of mixing chemicals for the processors. To Sherri, that much seemed pretty simple, and her running flow of questions soon induced a sigh of frustration from Mr. Vincent.

"Okay. We're going to take this thing from the top." He smiled in spite of himself. "When you walk into this room with a roll of film that you just took out of your camera, this is where you start." He walked to another processor on the far side of the room.

At the end of another hour, Sherri, for the first time, had a clear idea of how the prints were actually produced. "Will I be able to do all that?" She asked the question as she twisted herself into a strange contortion to look at the underside of an enlarger.

"When I say that you can." The supervisor brought her up short. "You'll have to convince me first that you'll remember how to do everything right. Ruining your own film would be one thing, but I draw the line at taking chances with expensive equipment. Okay?"

"Yes, sir." Sherri knew that. Her hands hadn't stopped shaking yet. But it was all so intriguing. Her fingers fairly itched to get started on some things of her own. She finished out her first day by helping Mr. Vincent run some strips of negatives through the processor.

Sherri was ecstatic when she left the office. One of the secretaries gave her a smile as she left. "Tired, Sherri? The first day is hard."

"Not a bit. I loved it!"

As she turned into the ranch driveway, she wondered absently whether she were a hazard on the road—an accident looking for a place to happen. She scarcely remembered anything about the drive home. Mentally she was still in the darkroom.

I wonder whether I could do superimposures, she thought, now that she knew the correct term for what she was thinking about. One picture printed on top of another. I know they can be done, but how hard is it? She had been turning that possibility over in her mind when she saw Kathleen's car. Immediately she felt the tension in her shoulders increase.

Once out of the car, she stood for a moment, hesitating. She didn't really want to go in. But then she saw someone pull the curtain aside in the living room. They'd heard her drive up. She paused again when she reached the door, put her hand on the doorknob, and took a deep breath.

Lynn and her father, Kathleen, Terry, and Kyle were all gathered in the living room. "Look who's here!" Sherri felt a surge of resentment at her father's affectionate reference to Kathleen.

Forcing a smile onto her face, Sherri made herself respond. "Hi, Kathleen. How are you doing?"

"Fine, thanks. It's good to be back. I hear you're a working girl now."

"Yes." Sherri couldn't think of anything else to say. Kathleen was as polished as Sherri remembered her. She wondered whether she'd ever be able to face the girl without feeling scruffy. "I didn't realize you were coming back so soon."

"No one did," Lynn commented. "Her friend's plans changed, so she decided to surprise us. I, for one, am sure not sorry!"

I am, Sherri thought. The greatly improved atmosphere of the past week seemed to disperse like a puff of mist.

"We were just talking about going for a ride, Sherri." Terry switched the subject. "Kathleen hasn't been up to Crest Spring yet, and it's supposed to be a beautiful sunset tonight. We're going to take a run up there before having a late supper. Do you want to come?"

"I, um." Sherri stopped. She most certainly did not want to go. But how could she say so? "I'm kind of tired, really. Maybe I'll just stay here." Again she arranged a smile on her face. "It will be a beautiful ride, Kathleen. Just don't let them push you too hard."

"Sherri?" Her father was looking at her in a special way he had that always made her nervous. "Have you ridden Sunny yet today?"

"No, sir."

"Yesterday?"

"No, sir."

"I think you'd better come along, riding him, that is. You promised you wouldn't let your duties here go slack."

Sherri clenched her jaw and looked down. It was several seconds before she managed the expected answer. "Yes, sir."

"We could wait a while if you'd like to rest first," Lynn said, seeming concerned.

"No," Sherri said brightly. "We might as well get going. I'll go get changed. See you at the barn."

Why postpone it, she thought on her way to her room. That's just more time to dread it. In spite of the fact that the others had been ready to go, Sherri still beat them to the barn. She had Sunny tacked up and ready to ride while they were still catching horses. So she managed to avoid most conversation by taking him into the breaking corral and working with him a little there while the rest finished their preparations.

Sunny was working well. He responded to the slightest shift of the reins and to her weight and legs as well. She put him into a lope and began working his circles smaller and tighter. Obligingly, he pulled his hindquarters in under him and swung his weight around on his hocks. A few more moments, and Sherri stopped him abruptly. "Ho!" she said sharply, taking the slack out of the reins for a moment. Sunny ground to a quick halt.

Sherri twisted in her saddle, scanned the ground and nodded her approval. In the dust of the corral, two distinct circles had been cut by Sunny's pounding hooves: one in a small, tight circle—from the back feet—and a slightly wider one, showing where the front feet had ranged around the back.

"He's about ready, isn't he?" Shane spoke from the gate.

"Yeah. I think so. I've been working him on cows for a month. I'm keeping up the dry work just to make him think."

"How are the lead changes? He used to hate the right lead."

"Better. Watch." Sherri touched Sunny's sides, and he sprang into a lope again. She swung him around in a circle to one side of the corral, then back to the middle. Responding to a slight shift of weight and one leg pressed against his girth, Sunny "skipped" a step in mid-stride, extending the opposite foreleg out first to carry his weight for the reversed direction. Making another circle, Sherri repeated the process, then again, and again.

"Nice," Shane admitted as Sherri brought the palomino to a halt again. "Dad has had a couple of people pestering him for a good horse. He'll probably let him go before long."

"He's ready," Sherri said with a shrug as she rode him out of the corral.

"He's beautiful, Sherri." Lynn rode near on the gray that her husband had mounted her on. "Did you train him?"

"Yes. I didn't break him, though. Shane did that."

"What's the difference?"

"Any horse you can get on without getting killed and make it go where you want is considered broke." Shane answered the question as he swung up on his big buckskin. " 'Trained' means to do the kind of stuff she was just making him do. Makes him worth something on a ranch."

"I see. Then one person usually doesn't do both?"

"Sometimes." Shane grinned. "But, personally, I find the training aspect boring as all get out. You do have to have a good horse to do ranch work, but it takes a lot of time and patience to help them figure out—and do—what you want. It's not my favorite. But I can ride circles around her on green broncs!"

"You can't either," Sherri retorted. "You just have to make yourself worthwhile somehow."

"Well, Lynn," Shane was unperturbed, "you can take whoever's version you like the best!" He cantered away to join Terry at the head of the group.

As they started out, Sherri stopped and dismounted to make an unnecessary adjustment to the girth of her saddle. That allowed her to drop behind the rest without being obvious. Straighten up, she told herself sternly. You're forgetting everything you've seen the Lord do in the last week—you're not being fair at all.

It didn't quiet the churning in her stomach, though, any more than scolding herself had ever helped before. "Help me to be patient enough to wait and see, Lord." Sherri actually spoke aloud—though softly. She didn't see what good could come of being around Kathleen, but then she had said the same about Lynn not too long ago.

She watched Kathleen for a while as the girl rode along between Shane and Lynn. It didn't take long for her to realize that Kathleen was as insecure on the horse as Sherri was around Kathleen. Though she was obviously going to great lengths not to make a show about it, Sherri wouldn't have been surprised to hear her say that she'd prefer the nearest air-conditioned jail to her seat in that saddle.

Sherri pushed that realization out of her mind. Following at a safe distance, she looked the other way and let her thoughts wander back to the darkroom. Her thoughts ran wild, realizing that she now had at least a faint possibility of being able to capture the beauty around her on film. It was just a question of learning how she was supposed to do it.

What a place, she thought, as they entered the higher country above the ranch buildings. She took a deep breath of the thin air. Late sunbeams were coming across the peaks in fiery blazes of gold. The slanted light plunged the east side of the mountains into darkness as it bathed the western slopes in radiant light. Below them the ranch stood out, the size of a child's railroad set, mere dark spots against the brilliant green of the spring grass. Far above, the Rocky Mountains towered, the steep slopes climbing between stands of aspen, dogwood, and spruce. Then came the timber line and the stark, slate blue barrenness above. Snow-capped peaks stood guard above the whole scene, glistening whiter than ever now with the glare from the setting sun.

Sherri had an eye for the scenery as she'd never had before. In her mind, she was framing one photo after another, wondering how a person was ever supposed to adjust exposures to capture the brilliant effects of the light as it really was.

Crest Spring itself had a new image for her. She stood at the edge of the pool and let Sunny drink, craning her neck to stare a hundred feet above. There, from the sheer rock wall of the canyon, poured a foaming jet of water. It fell in a roaring plunge to the deep pool below, boiling up again in apparent surprise at finding itself trapped.

Faintly, over the roar of the water, Sherri heard Lynn's and Kathleen's exclamations of delight. What would other people think if they could see this place? Sherri wondered. It's been on our private property since the United States was settled. Could I possibly do it justice on film?

"The spring is in the side of the mountain." Sherri could hear her father explaining the waterfall. "This is the lower side, so it's found it's way out here. It's a natural spring, fed from the melting snow up there." He gestured to the peaks. "It's been like this as long as anybody remembers. Probably a little wider, now, since the water would have worn away the rock. But I have pictures of my grandfather and father here when my dad was just a little boy."

Restoration! The thought leaped into Sherri's mind full-blown. What had Mr. Vincent been saying today about the technique for reproducing old photographs? She swung around to stare at her father. He was near the edge of the spring with Timmy, pointing upward in a gesture of explanation about something.

"Four generations," she mumbled. She could see the scene before her in a bright, color photograph. In a vignette of brown and white, as in a very old photo, there would be her grandfather and her great-grandfather, beside the same pool with the same background. "Could I do it?" She was unaware that she was speaking aloud.

"Do what?" Todd rode up beside her.

"What?" Sherri turned to look up at him, startled.

"What!" Todd frowned. "You look pretty strange just standing there talking to yourself. Could you do what?"

"Nothing that concerns you, buddy." Sherri hurriedly pulled herself aboard Sunny. "Dad!" She rode toward him. "Hey, Dad!"

"Yes?" He picked up his horse's reins and took a few steps toward her.

"Those pictures you were just talking about—where are they?"

He furrowed his brow in thought for a moment. "In the attic, somewhere, I would imagine. Probably in one of those old trunks."

"Would you mind if I looked for them?" Sherri didn't figure he would mind, but the trunks did belong to him.

"Of course not. Why?"

"Oh, I just got an idea." She paused and twisted around in her saddle, staring back the way they'd come, calculating the shortcuts required if she was going to beat the group back to the house.

"Dad?"

"Yes?"

"I'm going to take Sunny down the ridge trail. He needs the practice."

"Oh, Sherri, we can't take everybody down that way. The ride is too rough."

"I know. I'll just go ahead." She was already moving Sunny away. "I should be there before you, anyway, so if anything should go wrong, you'd know it right away when you get back."

Before he had any time to object, Sherri had pushed Sunny into a fast lope toward the far side of the canyon. Sunny objected slightly to leaving the other horses, and Sherri had to correct him several times before they entered the trail. The ridge trail, as they called it, cut straight down the side of the mountain that they had just come up. Instead of weaving back and forth on a grade and following the natural slopes of the mountain, it made a direct line straight south to the ranch.

Sherri pushed Sunny as fast as she dared in the gathering dusk. The descent was steep and often rocky. Several times Sunny had to bunch his hindquarters up and nearly sit down to keep his balance. Sherri helped him with weight, voice, and rein, but kept his pace brisk. Soon it grew too dark for her to see the flecks of lather forming on his coat, but she knew they were there.

Coming out on the last slope above the north pasture, she urged Sunny on even more. He increased speed and came down toward the gate in plunging, sliding bounds. Once into the pasture, Sherri made him walk the remaining half mile to the barn. By the time they got there, the gelding was at least partially cooled off. Sherri took care to finish cooling him properly. Even in her rush, she knew better than to take a chance on making a horse sick.

She was elated, however, that when she was finally able to turn Sunny loose, there was still no sign of the rest of the family. She left the barn on the run. Stopping at her room long enough to kick off her boots, she went into the hall and pulled down the stepladder that led to the attic.

The "attic" in their house was little more than a large crawl space. It was about the size of one of the bedrooms, and it was overflowing with clutter. Sherri groped her way through the darkness to find the string beneath the single light bulb. She blinked as the harsh light came on, then stared around for a few moments to orient herself.

EVERY PERFECT GIFT

There they were! Over in the back corner. Carefully, she began picking her way through the boxes and piles of unidentified paraphernalia. Two squarish, metal-bound footlockers sat near each other, one a dull black, the other a soupy green. Sherri scraped a clear spot on the floor before them and knelt down. Neither trunk was locked. She raised the lid on the large black one first. It contained an assortment of packages, clothing, and knick-knack keepsakes. A quick inspection of the contents told her that there were no photos.

When she opened the second trunk, there was no need to search. Envelope after envelope greeted her, standing in neat rows in old shoe boxes. Each envelope had a list of contents written on its front. Sherri rifled through, ignoring the ones marked as baby pictures, vacation of such-and-such, and Christmases of various years. Her flying fingers halted when she came across one envelope marked "negatives— wedding pictures."

"Wedding pictures?" She mumbled the question aloud, realizing that they had to be those of her dad and mother. Sherri opened the envelope enough for a quick peek inside. No photos. It was too dark up here to peer through the light and get a good glimpse of the images on the negatives.

Sherri had never seen wedding pictures of her mother, she realized with a start. There were very few photos or personal items of Debbie James around the house. Not that anyone had ever said there shouldn't be, but it had been mostly a tacit agreement by all the family members that it was easier not to remember too much.

Picking up the shoebox, Sherri decided she would continue the search in better light, where she could also get a good look at the negatives. Only when she saw what was beneath the shoebox did she realize that she'd started at the wrong place. Toward the bottom of the trunk, several aged photo albums lay stacked atop one another.

"Bingo!" Sherri discarded the shoe box and dug down to grasp the albums. Seating herself cross-legged on the floor, she flipped open the first cover and found herself looking at black and white photos of Rockview Ranch as it had been described to her years ago.

Time faded away from Sherri as she paged through the years that her grandfather had run their family ranch. When she came to the second album, she saw her father beginning to look the way that he looked now.

But not until she opened the third album did she stop short, her breath catching. A full-page photo leaped off the page, twisting her throat tight and bringing tears to her eyes. A bridal portrait of her mother. Even the swelling emotion didn't cushion Sherri's shock of seeing her own full, curly blonde hair and bright green eyes stare back at her from the picture.

You get more like your mother every day. Sherri heard her father's words again. A full minute passed before she slowly turned the page to see a piece of parchment sealed beneath plastic. "Believing marriage to be ordained and blessed of our Heavenly Father," Sherri read, half aloud, "Vincent and Heather Randen request the honor of your presence at the marriage of their daughter, Deborah Carese Randen, to Terrence Paul James. . . ."

Sherri continued on through the pages of photos of her father and mother. She was beautiful! Sherri had never really thought about her mother's appearance before, but the woman in the photographs before her was radiantly attractive. Sherri was dumbfounded by the similarity in their features. But there—honesty took over—the resemblance ended.

Even as the photos gave way to those of her parents' early years of marriage at the ranch, Sherri saw no picture where there was the slightest suggestion of roughness about her mother. Perfectly groomed to the last hair and the last fingernail, Debbie James stood out from the photos of her dark-haired husband and toddler sons. Sherri's first sensation, to her surprise, was a vague feeling of being let down.

The slamming of a door below brought her out of her reverie. Sherri flinched. She had no desire to put these pictures on display to the whole family. Instinctively, she knew that everyone would be upset by it. As for herself, Sherri was already upset. Hurriedly, she scooped up the entire stack of albums, balancing the shoebox on top of them, and made her way down the narrow ladder.

Sherri folded the ladder and swung it upward, returning it to its hiding place with a loud bang. Then she scurried for her room. She'd just barely have enough time to change and make it to supper. If she wasn't on time, there would be questions, and she wanted another uninterrupted chance to finish exploring her finds.

Chapter Fourteen

By late July, Sherri had almost forgotten that there had ever been any other way of life but what she was doing now. Every so often she would stop to wonder if the glow of her job would eventually wear off, but she didn't stay thinking about it very long. There were too many things to do and too many new possibilities to explore to waste time on introspection.

Somehow, in Sherri's preoccupation with her work, the tension she felt around Kathleen and Lynn seemed to fade. They just sort of blended in after a while. Probably, she realized dimly, her own foggy state of mind had as much to do with it as anything. Not to mention that Lynn and Kathleen were far more ready and willing than her brothers to help her out with any left-field photography projects she dreamed up. And not once did either of them tell her, in Terry's sterling words, that she ought to register herself as a nut and carry an ID card. "You have cameras on the brain, kid," he told her one day in embarrassed indignation when Sherri arrived home with a blown-up photo of him sleeping in the shade of a stand of aspens when he was supposed to have been checking fence lines.

He was probably right, she thought. Little by little, the darkroom was winning her interest. She still spent time with her sketch pads, but she was beginning to see that it would be years and years before professional results came through in her drawings. But the cameras were right here, right now. . . .

Sherri rarely left the Krayfor Agency without checking out one of the cameras. Her family had almost come to think of them as extensions of her arms. Sherri prowled the ranch with the cameras and a pad of paper for jotting down exposures and combinations that she wasn't sure about or wasn't sure she could remember. She took shot after shot of whatever caught her fancy. Sometimes she took a roll in a day; sometimes she spent half of the day itself agonizing over the arrangement of one or two frames. Most evenings found her in her room poring over photography and publishing journals that she borrowed from the various Krayfor employees. It took her half of an evening and half a dozen questions to Mr. Vincent the next day to nail down the difference between reflection of light and refraction of light—and what difference it made to her pictures. But Sherri was filled with a burning urgency to know everything about the profession that fascinated her so. She wanted to know how to do it better, quicker, clearer.

She showed Kathleen how to load a camera and made her practice so that she could do it in the time it took Sherri to shoot off another roll with the motor drive attachment on a second camera. Then she persuaded her stepsister to crawl beneath the loading chute with her, to where they could get the best view and the best pictures of Shane and Luke while they separated some of the young stock for an auction. Kathleen looked a little pained when they came out. She departed for a shower, taking a couple of swipes at the dust that covered her, but it didn't deter her from agreeing to a high-country ride for more photos the next day. Sherri knew she shouldn't go alone, and why not give this dude a riding lesson, to boot? Kathleen had been helpful to her, after all.

One evening not too long after that, Sherri was in her room when Kyle found her. "Hey, Sherri?"

"Hmm?" She answered absently without really looking up.

"What are you going to enter in the Trilton competition next week?" Kyle was asking about a local speed contest that was held near Rockview every year. A number of the trophies in both of their rooms had been won there.

"The what?"

"The Trilton contests!" Kyle's voice held a note of impatience.

"Oh. Yeah. I forgot." Sherri rolled over on her back and stared at the ceiling. "Wait a minute. That's next Saturday, isn't it?"

"Yeah."

"That's when Mrs. Vey said I could go to the wildlife painting exhibit with her if I wanted to." Sherri turned to look at him with a slightly apologetic expression. "I guess I won't be doing anything this time around."

"You what? You're crazy! We always—"

"I'm sorry, Kyle. But it's no matter, really. You guys will still ride. I really want to go to this show."

"You've got the best horse in the county for the pole races and you aren't even riding!" Kyle leaned a shoulder against the doorway, disgust evident in his voice.

"Well, he's my own. I trained him, too; so I'm not robbing anybody. Don't get pushy." Sherri flipped back on her stomach and reopened her magazine.

Kyle was silent for a moment. "You never do anything with us, anymore, Sherri."

Sherri looked up, surprised. "I do too."

"Not like you used to. Everything's different." His frown was growing. "When everybody else griped about their sisters, I used to tell them that you were more fun than any of my brothers. But any more, you act just like—like a girl."

Sherri laughed out loud, and immediately wished she hadn't. Kyle looked away, his face flushed slightly red.

"Why don't you ride Sprint?" Sherri wondered what it would take now to make peace.

His head jerked up. "Why?"

"Well? Who else is going to? I'm not. You might as well. You'd probably ride him better anyway." Sherri turned back to her magazine. Somehow the conversation was beginning to get dull.

"You mean you wouldn't mind?" Kyle was obviously amazed. Sherri didn't stop to think that not too many weeks ago she would have threatened to break the legs of anyone who even thought about climbing onto her trophy-attracting horse.

"Why should I?" Sherri was half-absorbed in her article.

"Well. . . ." Kyle's voice trailed away. "Wow. You are really, I mean you are . . . wow." He shook his head and left the room.

Sherri raised her head for a moment. Now why did I do that, she wondered. A brief thought of the excitement of the competition rose in her mind. For a moment she frowned; then shrugging her shoulders, she turned back to the magazine.

It was a graphic-arts specialty publication. This particular issue had an article in it titled "101 Thoughts for Originality in Lettering." Sherri had been thinking in a whole new direction ever since the night she'd found the old family albums in the attic. One of the bulky volumes had turned out to be not a photograph album at all, but a storage notebook for a large quantity of her mother's artwork. Eureka! She'd hardly been able to keep from exclaiming aloud. Why didn't I ever think about this before? In spite of knowing that her mother had been a professional artist, Sherri had never stopped to think about where all the samples of her work had disappeared to.

She was careful not to mention anything to her father, however, instinctively knowing that seeing or discussing the pieces would be hard on him. But Sherri spent hours with the notebook. It was crammed to bursting with calligraphy, illustrations, rough sketches, and finished pieces. There was a bold flair to her mother's work that Sherri envied as she compared it to her own timid attempts. One of the calligraphy pieces had so captivated her that she had taken it from the notebook and put it in place of a picture of Taffy that once sat in a beautiful wooden frame on her dresser.

"Every good gift and every perfect gift is from above, and cometh down from the Father of lights, with whom is no variableness, neither shadow of turning." James 1:17. The ornate script lettering, in flawless perfection, flowed across the white parchment in a blended pattern of blue, gold, and black. It stirred a memory that was buried deep in Sherri's mind.

Hadn't that been one of her mother's favorite passages? Sherri struggled to remember more clearly, but the thought remained only a vague impression. Well, anyway, Mother liked it well enough to do a lettering piece with it. Sherri had carried the frame to the central place of honor on her bookshelf. Nearby, she'd added the notebook full of her mother's work to the stack of sketch pads and drawings that she'd cherished for so long.

But that evening Sherri's thoughts returned to Kyle again several times. Funny, she mused. I don't really think there've been that many changes. She was reluctant to give it too much thought, somehow, or even to examine her reasoning for why she didn't want to.

It was several days later, though, that not only Kyle but nearly all the rest of the family decided she definitely had lost her mind. Sherri was just finishing the supper dishes when she heard the phone ring. Shane's voice answered it in the hall outside the den.

"Hello? Hi. . . . Um-hmm. . . . Oh, really? . . . Great. You got to be kidding. I guess I know what we'll be doing tomorrow. . . . Yeah, we have a herd up by Pine Bench. . . . Okay, thanks. We'll let you know. Bye."

Sherri hung up the dishtowel and scurried to the den. Whatever it was sounded interesting. She entered just in time to hear Shane reporting to their dad. "That was Joe Rawlins."

Her father nodded. The Rawlins ranch was next to Rockview on the west side. Shane continued. "They had their plane out today and spotted the stallion and his bunch on the north boundary. He figured we'd want to know."

Their father flung his newspaper on the floor. "Ahh, that dumb horse!"

Sherri felt a thrill shoot all the way up her spine.

Her dad stood up. "Well, let's make plans for an early morning ride. We've got to run that buzzard out before he makes off with our whole herd."

"Dad!" Sherri didn't even stop to wonder about what he'd think. "Can I please ride up there tonight and get some pictures before you run them off?"

"What?" He froze in place, as though he couldn't believe what he'd heard.

"Pictures! I have the zoom lens home tonight and everything—I don't have to have it back for three days. And I've told Mrs. Vey so much about the herd. I have shots of almost everything else around here except some of Pharitell, and I could get them before you ran them off in the morning and—"

"Sherri!" He had to raise his voice to cut in on her. "Slow down. I can't make top nor bottom out of whatever you're trying to say. I can't even find a middle."

She took a deep breath and clutched her arms across her stomach. "I've been taking a lot of pictures of the ranch this summer."

"I've noticed."

Sherri didn't miss the dryness of his tone, but she ignored it and rushed on. "One thing I've always really wanted was to get some good shots of the wild herd and Pharitell. Except I didn't think I'd ever have a chance. But now they're here. If I could get up there tonight, I could get some first thing in the morning before you run them off the ranch."

"You can't possibly go up there tonight." Her dad still looked a little bewildered. "And what do you want pictures of that infernal outlaw for, anyway?"

"Shane would go with me, wouldn't you?" Sherri whirled on him with a smile, preferring to ignore her father's second objection.

"Huh? I don't want to go on any all-night ride just for some dumb. . . ." His voice trailed away as Sherri took a step toward him.

"Please, Shane? Please? Just for me? I'll ride the red colt for you for the rest of the summer. Please?"

He stared at her for a long moment. No one moved or said anything. Shane mumbled something to himself and dropped into a chair. Then he looked up at his father, who in turn looked at Lynn.

Lynn just laughed softly, shrugging her shoulders. "Sounds like a ranch decision to me."

Her dad sat down again. He stared at Sherri for what seemed like a long time. "You really want pictures of that troublemaker?"

She nodded vigorously. "He's beautiful, Dad. You know that. Even if he is a pain. He's exactly what people have all the exotic ideas about—you know, the wild stallion. Especially a white one."

"He's a gray." He looked totally befuddled.

"Yeah. But he looks white from a distance. That's what dudes call 'white' anyway."

Her father looked at Lynn again, then back at Sherri. "Well, I guess I don't know why you can't. If Shane will go with you."

Shane nodded, if a little reluctantly, before their father went on. "But we're leaving here at four tomorrow morning. I'm not waiting on any camera lens once I get up there. I'll not have that stallion in with my brood mares."

"Yes, sir." Sherri whirled around and started for the kitchen. "Shane, if you'll get the horses ready, I'll pack whatever else we'll need."

Shane sighed and leaned his head back. "I have a crazy sister!" he shouted, before heaving himself to his feet.

Sherri just smiled as she heard him bang out of the house.

Chapter Fifteen

"There's even a moon," Sherri commented as they picked their way onto the Crest Ridge trail.

"So? It's a good thing. We'd have twice the trouble if there weren't one."

"I know. But it's good for photos. Not quite full, but the light will be about the same."

"You're going to try to take pictures at night?"

Sherri could tell he really didn't believe her. "Yep. I have all kinds of different film. Even some thousand-speed, plus a tripod. You can do it. You just have to be careful, or you can wind up with really grainy-looking prints."

"Grain-ee?"

"Yeah. It looks like the picture was printed on rough paper or something. Almost a textured look if it gets bad enough."

"Oh."

"I'll want to get some shots in the light, of course, but as long as we're up here, I might as well try night, too."

"As long—girl, I thought I saw bedrolls on these horses. I'm planning on getting some sleep."

"Sleep if you want to. I'm going to take pictures."

"I can't let you go wandering off. Dad will scalp me."

"Huh. I know that area as well as you do. Besides, if you spook that herd, I'll scalp you myself."

"Huh." Shane returned the scoff. "As if you can sneak up on them any better than me."

That topic of conversation dropped as the increasingly difficult trail demanded their attention. Fortunately, the horses knew the trail as well as Shane and Sherri. They didn't talk much for the next few hours, but they made good time. Even Sherri would have had to admit that she felt tired, but she was also thrilled over the chance that was staring her in the face.

By the time they neared the trail below Pine Bench, Sherri could see by the illuminated dial on her watch that it was fifteen minutes past one. "How much farther do you suppose we should ride?" She was careful to keep her voice low. They couldn't see far, and both knew there would be no sneaking up on the stallion if Pharitell had any idea they were around.

"Probably we're about far enough. Rawlins said they were headed this way, and they were across the line when he spotted them."

"All right. Let's look for a good spot."

"Why don't we just take the horses to the line cabin? We're close enough—we can leave them there."

Sherri thought for a moment. "Okay. Let's go." Less than a mile from where they were was a rough, one-room cabin, put up to shelter anyone who had to make an overnight trip to the far corner of the ranch. There was also a small corral. It wasn't big, but generally there was enough grass growing in it to keep horses satisfied for a little while. They wouldn't be likely to call out to another bunch or try too hard to get out to join them.

After they'd turned the horses loose, they sat for a while to rest their legs and backs. "Whew." Sherri heaved a sigh. "I'm out of shape."

"You ought to be." Shane grunted. "You've hardly been up here all summer. You have yourself cloistered away at that agency forty-eight hours a day."

Sherri was silent. She stretched out on her back and looked up. The moon stood out in its brilliant fullness. It flooded the slopes and mountain peaks with pale, white light, accenting the millions of huge, glittering stars that stared down at her. She shivered and pulled her coat tighter around her. The mountain nights were cold, even in the middle of the summer.

"I love what I'm doing, Shane," she commented finally.

"Yeah. I know." Shane shifted his position to lean against a corral post. "It's just hard to get used to. You've changed a lot."

"What do you mean?" Sherri sat halfway up. "I'm gone a lot, I know, but nothing's really different."

"Yes, it is. You're different."

"I am not!"

"Don't be so touchy. I mean it in a good way. I hoped something would happen. Remember? I said so earlier this summer. I just didn't think about anything like this."

Sherri leaned back to gaze at the sky again. She didn't say anything else.

There was a fairly long silence before Shane went on. "You act more like a girl, Sher. There's nothing wrong with that. I know I teased you before Lynn and Kathleen came, but I really think it's done you good. Lynn, I mean. There's a lot you needed to learn."

"You're always blunt, aren't you?"

Sherri didn't miss his answering shrug. "At least you know I mean what I say."

Silence followed. In spite of their intentions to rest only for a few minutes and in spite of the chill, both of them dozed off. The ride up had been long and hard. Sherri wasn't sure how much time had passed when they both jerked awake at once.

"Listen!"

Sherri's exclamation was unnecessary. Neither of them could possibly have missed the clarion call of the stallion.

It echoed and rebounded from the rocky slopes above, so shrill in pitch that it was almost a whistle.

"He's close!" Shane's voice was a whisper.

"Let's go." Sherri was already digging in her saddlebag. They divided the equipment between them and set off toward the north.

"I bet they're in the basin," Shane said softly. Sherri was amused by the note of excitement in his voice.

What a typical guy, she thought. He'd die before he'd let me think I had a good idea in coming up here.

But she confined her response to "Yeah. That would give me the perfect chance to set the camera up on the south side. On the ridge."

"That far away?"

"I have a really strong lens for the camera. If they're in the basin, it'll be all right."

Twenty minutes later, they were creeping up the slope on the far side of Pine Bench. Scarcely daring to breathe, Sherri followed Shane as he crawled on all fours across the top of the ridge to a small covering of aspen trees. There below them, in the meadow drenched by moonlight, was a huge herd of horses. Sherri had to search for a full minute before she spotted Pharitell. He stood on a knoll to the northwest of the herd. Motionless, he held his head high, testing the wind.

Once again, his challenging call rang out through the night. Sherri jumped. She almost yelped from the surprise of it.

"Shh!" Shane cautioned. "He hasn't picked up our scent, but the ole' sixth sense is telling him that everything isn't kosher."

"Well, I have some pictures to get before he figures it out." Working as swiftly as possible, but giving priority to absolute quiet, Sherri pulled out her tripod and set it up. By the light of Shane's tiny penlight, she loaded the correct film into the camera.

Fastening the camera to the top of the tripod, she experimented with the three different lenses that she had brought.

"What are you fussing about?" Shane could contain himself no longer.

"I'm trying to make sure I'm doing this right. The exposures, I mean. I'm not going to get a second chance, you know." Sherri crouched over the camera, peering through the viewfinder, watching the electronic displays inside the camera. When she thought she was satisfied, she began snapping pictures. Shane gave up and stretched out on the ground again as Sherri crept back and forth on the ridge, dragging camera and tripod with her, trying to follow the movements of Pharitell as he kept a strict guard over his herd.

Sherri tried every combination of exposure and shutter speed that she could think of. She tried the same shots again and again, not sure whether the stallion had moved during the extended time that the shutter was open. A pink hue was lighting the eastern sky before Sherri crawled back to Shane.

"I'm going down closer before it gets so light that I can't make it without him seeing me."

Shane had been asleep again. It took him a minute to get oriented. "Okay." His voice was resigned. "Hey, let me see that for a sec before you go. Maybe I can get a better view."

He took the camera and heavy lens from her. Holding it up, he scanned the herd below. "Uh-oh."

"What?"

"Terrific. Sherri, look again. At the herd, this time, not the stallion."

"I've been taking as many of the herd as of him, but—" Sherri's voice broke off as she focused the camera again in the growing light. On the edge of the herd closest to her was Dusty, their father's old cutting horse. Looking a little further, she spotted Dutch and Rocky. A groan escaped her. "Our mares!"

"Sure enough our mares." Shane was moving back already. "Sherri, I've got to go down and meet Dad so he'll know where they are. We'll have to do some fancy footwork to cut those mares out before they all take off."

"All right. I'm still going down there."

"Fine. Just stay away from that stallion. I'll leave Taffy at the cabin. We'll meet you back there afterward."

Sherri reloaded with a more appropriate speed of film and began a careful descent, taking advantage of every shred of cover she could find. She made it to the grove below, about three hundred yards from the herd. She couldn't believe Pharitell hadn't spotted her or scented her until she realized that he was engaged in an argument with one of the young colts.

"Thank you, Lord," Sherri breathed, knowing that probably nothing else would have sufficiently distracted the herd boss. The colt was nearing the age when he would be driven out of the herd as a threat to the stallion.

She took a few shots from her new point of view but soon discovered that the light wasn't really cooperating. The beams of the rising sun were straight toward her, and the herd still too far away. Well, I'll just have to wait for something to change, she thought. It would be dumb to go any closer. He'd smash me like a plum just for the fun of it.

The sun rose higher and higher. Sherri's legs were cramped and stiff. Every muscle in her body screamed for release from her enforced hiding place. But still she kept her gaze riveted on the herd. A few times, she'd been able to snap a fast shot as some of the horses wandered on this side of the herd, but she had to be careful about how much movement she made. Clearly, Pharitell was restless and ready to move on, except that this time of day was feeding time for most horses that run loose. Even the alert stallion was snatching mouthfuls of grass.

Suddenly a shout rang out from the far end of the basin. Sherri jumped from her own surprise, but her reaction was nothing compared to that of the stallion. With a wild cry, he swept down on his herd, panicking them into an instant stampede.

Suddenly the meadow seemed to be full of riders. From the north, south, and from the entry to the basin they came. Sherri's father had planned carefully and quickly. He'd figured the stallion would make for the ranch mares, so he'd rounded up the manpower to do something about it.

The meadow was full of cracking whips, whistles, and shouts. In a few moments, Sherri had sorted out Shane, Terry, Kyle, Dandy, Luke, and Rick, as well as their neighbor, Joe Rawlins, and his three sons.

Pharitell tried in vain to stampede his herd through the two openings into the basin, but both were sufficiently blocked by riders. By himself, the stallion could easily have run through. No one would have dared to challenge him. But he wouldn't leave the mares, who, in their panic, refused to face the men and the cracking whips.

For the space of ten minutes there was mass confusion. Or at least it looked that way to Sherri. But she knew what was happening. Little by little, a herd gathered at the far end. She could tell that the ranch horses were being separated from the wild bunch. Then came a long, drawn-out whistle, repeated twice more. On signal, the riders at Sherri's end of the basin moved away from the entry. In an instant, Pharitell spotted the opening.

Another electric surge went through Sherri as she realized that the whole herd was coming right toward her. Frantically she checked the film in her camera and then raced for the windfall of birch trees on the other side of the small stream nearby. She had to get up on something, quickly, or she'd get trampled.

Pulling herself up on a wide birch trunk that sat four feet off the ground, Sherri began focusing and snapping shots as the herd thundered toward her. They reached the stream and charged across it, knocking sheets of water high into the morning sunlight. Mares, foals; young, old; big, small. She was almost out of film when the stallion came through.

She had figured he would spot her, but she hadn't expected an outright challenge. He leaped out of the stream and dug to a halt fifty feet away. He reared and struck out with his front legs, shrilling his call loudly enough to make Sherri feel as though her eardrums were bursting.

"Dear Lord, don't let him come any closer!" Sherri's hands were shaking badly, but not too much to keep her from taking a couple more shots. Time hung in suspension for a moment as she wondered whether or not Pharitell was going to charge her. The herd decided for him. As the last of them pounded by, the stallion gave a snort and raced away to catch up. Creepers! she thought. He was a lot bigger than she'd imagined him to be. She waited a moment, then slid from the tree trunk to stand on shaky legs.

"You crazy kid!" Sherri looked up to see Terry cantering toward her. "What were you doing in there? Shane said you promised to stay out of the way."

"Yeah. Except he didn't tell me you guys were bringing in a whole squadron. I didn't know what you were going to do."

"You should have known."

"Well, I got my pictures, anyway!" Sherri was much too elated to even recognize that she was being chewed out. "Look—six rolls!"

"So what! Come on, let's get out of here. I'm hungry."

Sherri swung up behind him, and they cantered away to join the others.

Chapter Sixteen

Sherri lost no time in getting to the Agency darkroom the next day. It was Saturday, so nearly the entire office was deserted. She thought that was all the better as she paused in the darkroom to collect her thoughts. She took a couple of deep breaths and waited a few moments before starting to run the film through the processor. This was no time to make a mistake because she was rushing or not being careful.

The automatic processor ran the film through very quickly, but it wasn't fast enough for Sherri. She had to restrain herself from yanking the negatives out as they began to come through the feeder. Sherri grabbed the first strip and slapped it into the enlarger. She flicked on the light and began to run the frames through, watching the projected image on the white counter beneath. Strip after strip—Sherri wasn't even aware that she started to slow down, caught up in the absorption of studying the negatives.

Slowly, something was beginning to prick at the back of her mind. She had wanted the pictures just as much for herself as for anything. The horses were beautiful, and she had always loved to tell people about them. She'd been noncommittal to her father's questions about the outcome of the photo session. But as she studied the results of her night in the Pine Bench meadow, she began to wonder if maybe, just maybe, she might have done a decent job.

She stopped altogether when she put the last strip of negatives in the enlarger, and then she stood a long time staring at the image projected on the countertop. The shot was of Pharitell. He stood on the knoll where she'd first seen him. Head drawn high, ears pricked, and nostrils flared, he was searching the night for threats to his herd. His coat glistened nearly silver in the flooding light from the moon; his mane and tail were both whipped to one side, in the same direction as the waving of the grass.

Just below him on the slope lay a small foal. Sherri hadn't even noticed it while she'd been taking the pictures. It was darker in color than Pharitell and sprawled full length on the grass. In the background, above the stallion's head, the moon stood out against the blackness, throwing a discernable shadow that pointed toward the foal, stopping just short of its head.

Sherri sighed. "Oh, boy," she said quietly. Sherri spent several minutes playing with the exposures and timers on the enlarger, but finally she reached into a drawer and pulled out an eight- by ten-inch piece of paper. She snapped it into a frame and positioned it on the counter. She hit the switch, waited, then fed the paper into the other processor.

Time seemed to stop while Sherri waited for the print to appear. She snatched it up and hurried to the fully lit viewing room. Critically she inspected the picture: focus, contrast, composition. She paused and looked up for a moment, as though afraid to face what she was thinking. But suddenly, with a rush of conviction, Sherri knew that she was holding a very good shot.

Sherri felt her face flush and her pulse rate pick up. When she looked back at the photo, she realized her hands were shaking. I did it, she thought. I really, really did it! A ridiculously huge grin was forcing its way across her face. She stood there, lost in thought for another few minutes, then made her way slowly back through the darkroom to the main office.

She'd come out to see if she could find anyone at all, but to her delight, she saw that the door to Mrs. Vey's office was open. She crossed the room and timidly tapped on the partly open door.

"Yes?" Mrs. Vey looked up from where she was seated at her desk. "Why, Sherri! I didn't know you were here. Whatever brings you in here on a Saturday afternoon?"

"I, um. I got a chance to get some pictures, and I wanted to get them processed." Sherri stood barely inside the door, holding the print low at her side.

"Important photos, hmm?" Mrs. Vey's smile was as steady as always.

"Yes, ma'am. I thought—that is, well, would you. . . . I'd like you to see this." Swiftly, before she could lose her nerve, Sherri stepped forward and laid the print on Mrs. Vey's desk. The lady looked down at the photo.

The art director froze for the briefest of moments, staring at the shot of Pharitell. Then she picked it up slowly. As Sherri waited in suspense, she could hear the ticking of a clock somewhere.

Mrs. Vey glanced at her, then back down, so quickly that Sherri almost missed it. When the lady finally opened her mouth to speak, there was, again, just the briefest hesitation before she actually said anything. "Sherri, this is quite good."

Sherri felt the blood pounding in her ears again, and the grin began tugging at the corners of her mouth once more.

"Are there other shots?" Mrs. Vey finally looked up to meet her eyes.

"Yes, ma'am." The grin won. "I took six rolls—everything I had home with me. I didn't have time to come after anything else. At least I had a fairly decent selection of film there."

"May I see the rest?" Mrs. Vey rose from the chair, still holding the print.

"Sure. They're in the darkroom still. I just finished processing." Sherri led the way. "A lot of it's not worth anything at all. I was really taking some wild guesses about exposures for some of the night shots, but there are four or five that I kind of like."

Mrs. Vey didn't comment. She went to the enlarger that Sherri indicated and began scanning the negatives. Sherri seated herself on a stool near the processor and pulled herself into the tiniest knot possible. She scarcely dared to breathe while her boss continued the inspection.

For a full fifteen minutes, Mrs. Vey was totally absorbed in the strips of film. Then she turned around and leaned back on the counter. She studied Sherri for a few moments. "Sherri, I would like to see you explore the possibility of entering some of those photos in the Kiston Junior Photographers Show."

Sherri still didn't move—much less did she speak. She'd been hoping for a few words of praise. A commendation for some good composition and good judgment with the exposures. But a photography show? She couldn't think of anything to say. Finally she pushed a question out. "Like the show we were at last week?"

"Very much like it," Mrs. Vey answered. "Except, of course, that it was an exhibition by professional artists. This is strictly amateur exhibits by photographers under twenty years of age."

Sherri remained silent.

"It's not a sales exhibit. It would be just a chance at the recognitions they give." Mrs. Vey began explaining a little further. "Just as in the show last week, there are a variety of awards and runner-ups given, and a number of honorable mentions, and the like. It's an excellent chance to get a little exposure for yourself and to see how you compare with other people who have your interests."

"You really think I should?"

"I'd hardly have recommended it if I didn't think so."

Sherri thought hard for a moment. "Mrs. Vey?"

"Yes?"

"How many—I mean, some of the exhibits we saw last week were groups of paintings done around a particular theme. Do they do that at the Kiston Show?"

"Yes." Mrs. Vey thought for a moment. "You can enter your pieces as a group exhibit rather than as individuals, but they do have to be part of a group. They have to have a 'theme,' as you said. Generally there is a title given to the group as well as to the individual pieces. What are you thinking of, Sherri?"

"A presentation of the ranch." The words burst out of Sherri in a rush. "I've been taking pictures all summer, mostly just because I was so fascinated with it. There have been some things that have turned out fairly well, I think. But then a few weeks ago, well, I found some old photos and negatives from when my grandpa and great-grandfather used to run the ranch, and I've been trying to do superimposures of them onto current pictures of the same places, and—"

"Sherri!" For the second time that afternoon, Mrs. Vey seemed to be a little short on words. Sherri began to be afraid that her boss was angry with her until she spoke again.

"I'd like to see the things you've been working on. Will you bring them with you on Monday?"

"Yes, ma'am." Sherri nodded vigorously.

"Good. I'd like to discuss this with you further, but I'm going to be late for an appointment if I don't hurry."

Sherri wasn't conscious of feeling tired on the way home, as she mentally reviewed the negatives she'd looked through. In her mind's eye, she was setting up her exhibit for the Kiston Show—an idea that set her mind afire, part exhilaration and part terror that she'd embarrass herself. Sherri thought of the hundreds of photos she'd taken over the summer: shots of the little boys, of her older brothers, her father, Lynn, the horses, the property. With a jolt Sherri realized that she had only a few weeks until school started. She'd have to work fast, because once she was back in classes, she knew she'd have very little extra time to spend at Krayfor.

"Oh, boy," she said for the second time that day.

She was still in a state of euphoria at dinner. It was a reflection of her state of mind that she didn't object to Lynn's suggestion as they finished the dishes.

"Why don't you wear your new dress to church tomorrow, Sherri? It's late enough in the summer, and it's been cool enough so that it shouldn't be too warm."

"All right," she agreed absently, not really thinking too much about it. Most of her mind was already back in the darkroom, sorting and reframing pictures.

The next morning, however, reality returned with a thud. She'd taken the greatest care she knew how in every aspect of her appearance. And the dress was no disappointment— Sherri was startled all over again by what it did for her coloring. But when it came to the hair.... She finally dropped into the chair before the vanity mirror, heaving a sigh of despair. Glancing to the side, she stared forlornly at the newly framed wedding portrait of her mother.

Sherri resumed her struggles, trying to brush the curly mass into some semblance of order. Five minutes later, she was near tears of frustration.

"Sherri?" She heard Lynn's voice from the hall. "Could I get you to help me with something?"

Sherri didn't answer. Her throat was too tight. Suddenly she was angry as she saw her stepmother enter the room with every hair and thread in exact place.

"Sherri?"

Sherri still didn't answer.

"What's wrong?"

Sherri dropped her brush on the vanity top and pressed her fingers on either side of the bridge of her nose in an effort to stop the tears. She was aware of the heavy silence behind her as Lynn studied her reflection in the mirror. Sherri refused to meet her eyes.

"Just a moment." Lynn turned for the door. "I'll be right back."

Sherri barely had time to heave a shaky sigh to release a little tension before Lynn reappeared, carrying several bulky items in her arms. "These are still hot. I just finished with them." She was setting down a box of hot rollers and a brush curling iron.

Leaning down beside the vanity, Lynn sought out the electrical socket and plugged them in. "Now, let's—"

"I don't think—" Sherri started to interrupt and tried getting to her feet, but Lynn grabbed her shoulders and pushed her down.

"Hush. Sit down, now. Give me ten minutes and I'll leave you alone."

More rapidly than Sherri could follow what she was doing, Lynn deftly separated her stepdaughter's blonde mop into sections and wound it onto the rollers. She spent a few brief moments with the brush curling iron on the shorter layers of bangs, then popped the rollers out. Putting the brush down, Lynn snatched up a wide hair lift and began picking at the full, tumbling curls that now hung around Sherri's head. With a quick swish Lynn created a side part, swirling the hair up away from Sherri's face on the full side, and catching it back with a gold hair comb on the off side. The curls were only too eager to cooperate, standing out in all their body and strength.

Sherri stared at her reflection, transfixed.

"You have lovely hair, Sherri." Lynn's hand was still resting on Sherri's shoulder. "Do you have any curlers?"

"Yes." Sherri spoke in a low voice. "Aunt Lindy sent me some a year or so ago, but I've never used them. I always thought my hair was curly enough."

"You should use them. It gives some control to whatever you try to do with your hair—even as curly as it already is. See?"

Slowly, Sherri nodded. Even more slowly, she stood up, almost as though she were afraid she would jar the image in the mirror and make it disappear. At the same time she felt a little embarrassed, thinking of how she'd always detested the girls who spent most of the noon hour primping in the bathroom. Yet, honesty stopped her thoughts. She knew there was a difference between that sort of thing and the attitude her stepmother showed.

A moment later Sherri was sure that Lynn was able to read her mind. "The Lord has given you some beautiful features, Sherri. There's absolutely nothing wrong with making the most of yourself. As long as it doesn't become your primary focus. The 'inward beauty' has to match." Lynn patted her shoulder slightly. "We are the actual temples of God, Sherri. And look at the beauty in the world that the Lord created. There's no fault in doing what we can—in fact it's a matter that directly affects our testimonies. When was the last time you read Proverbs 31?"

With that, Lynn left. Sherri quickly pulled herself together and followed her to the kitchen. She knew that Tim and Todd would still need help getting ready, and with her mind on that, she was totally unprepared for her older brothers' reactions. If they had teased her, she could have dealt with it better. Shane's response was undoubtedly the most out-standing. She could hear him coming from halfway down the hall. He was yelling something back at Todd.

"You are not bringing that dumb tape this morning. I had to listen to it all the way to church and back last week. If you have to bring it, you can ride with Dad."

An unintelligible reply came back from Todd.

"I don't care! You—" Shane broke off and stopped abruptly as he saw Sherri. She had Timmy standing on a chair by the sink while she slicked his hair down. Shane stared at Sherri. "Wow," he said quietly. "That's nice."

"Thanks." She responded without looking up. From the corner of her eye she could see Lynn's smile. Was it amusement, Sherri wondered? She risked a more direct glance at her stepmother and realized with a start that it was just plain satisfaction.

Sherri's mind was still chewing on that late in the evening after the night service was over. Back in her room, she lay on her bed and stared at the ceiling. She heard her pastor's words from the sermon again. "Don't underestimate God's power in your life, friend. He controls what's happening. Your choice is only to submit to His control or to resist—only to choose whether He will use you for a good example or for a bad example."

Well, somebody besides me has sure been controlling things in the last few months, Sherri thought. I couldn't have dreamed all this up if I were an eccentric little old lady with a quill pen.

Sherri stared upward for a few more moments. Then suddenly she rolled over, pulled her Bible from the bedside table, and searched the Old Testament pages until she reached Proverbs 31. Propping herself up on one elbow, she began to read. The familiar verses leaped off the page as though she'd never seen them before. The farther she read, the stronger grew a picture in her mind: *She is not afraid of the snow for her household: for all her household are clothed with scarlet. She maketh herself coverings of tapestry; her clothing is silk and purple. . . . Strength and honour are her clothing; and she shall rejoice in time to come. She openeth her mouth with wisdom: and in her tongue is the law of kindness. . . .*

Sherri stopped and flopped back on the bed. *In her tongue is the law of kindness. . . . Strength and honour are her clothing.* What better description of her stepmother could she have written herself? *The law of kindness. . . .* In spite of everything, had Lynn ever showed any resentment? Had she ever demonstrated anything but a concern for those around her?

Things couldn't have been easy for Lynn, Sherri finally admitted. Especially with Todd and Timmy driving her up the wall at every opportunity—at least until she'd learned to crack down on them. In all of Sherri's worrying this spring, she thought, when had she ever stopped to consider the fact that Lynn, herself, might feel awfully inadequate for what she was faced with? Yet, look at her. And listen to her. There was no getting away from the words Sherri had just read—this was God's own description of a woman who was on the right track! In a single moment, Sherri felt a flush cover her whole face. What a contrast between us, she thought dismally.

Sherri's gaze shifted to the ornate frame on the shelf beside her: "Every good gift and every perfect gift is from above, and cometh down from the Father. . . . " Somehow, she'd always thought of that verse in the sense that people talk about "spiritual gifts." And she supposed that was true. But special gifts from God clearly took many forms. For the first time, Sherri realized that even without the job she wouldn't want to turn the clock back.

"And You knew it all the time, Lord." Sherri felt a new and unusual sense of security as she whispered aloud. "Thank you. I really mean it this time. Thank you for sending her." Sherri's thoughts continued without prompting. But how in the world can I ever tell her "thank you"? What words would ever make her understand what I'm thinking?

Chapter Seventeen

The days of late summer sped by. Sherri thought frequently about her resolve to talk to Lynn, but every time they were alone together, Sherri found herself tongue-tied. She tried to find new ways to be especially nice to both Lynn and Kathleen, though. She coached their riding and went out of her way to strike up casual conversation whenever she could. Sherri was getting in the habit of checking with Kathleen before she went for a ride to see whether her stepsister wanted to go. One such day, Sherri headed for Kathleen's room to ask her and was thunderstruck to find her in tears—upset, of all things, by a session of teasing from Todd and Kyle. Sherri's mind rocked at the realization that the family's mental roughhousing would hit anyone that hard.

"I'm sorry, Sherri!" Kathleen had smiled in spite of herself. "I know they're just kidding around. But it's hard to get used to." Sherri resisted the urge to go find Kyle and Todd and bang their heads together. But from then on, she was fast to take Kathleen's part in the verbal fencing matches.

"You sent them to me, Lord," Sherri prayed one night. "I'm really beginning to see that. Please help me as I try to understand the things You're teaching me. Help me to remember how uncomfortable others might be before I worry about myself." And her own prayer was strangely true. Sherri began to find that by the time she finished being concerned about how Kathleen was feeling, she'd often forgotten to feel uncomfortable herself.

When it came time to buy school clothes that year, Sherri isolated herself for several days behind the locked door of her room. No need to have to put up with her brothers' harassment, she reasoned while she fought through several long sessions with the hot rollers until she managed to get the idea. Then she went through her closet like a small tornado, sorting, trying on, and experimenting. She thought back to Lynn's early summer comments about matching clothes-coloring to people-coloring and attacked dressing every morning with the same approach that she would have used with a drawing. And when the shopping trips came, Sherri made certain that both Lynn and Kathleen were along.

But nothing was capable of keeping Sherri's thoughts away from the upcoming photography show for very long. Most of her days were spent in a fever of activity: planning, printing, retaking last shots, or fussing over mats and frames. Sometimes Sherri felt as though she were going to come apart before the strain was all over. How am I ever going to cope with the weeks between my entry and the opening of the show, she wondered. Waiting patiently had never been her strong point, and she was anticipating a lot of wall-climbing. Somehow, Sherri had come to think of the show as her proving ground. Would she be good enough to continue? Had she learned enough to justify what she was doing? How would her work compare with the work of others who had such a head start on her?

Mrs. Vey was quick to point out that one show wasn't the beginning or the ending of everything. "It's just a measuring stick, Sherri. The whole world isn't hanging on the outcome. This will just give you a good idea of where you stand and what your strengths—and possibly your weaknesses—are."

Nonetheless, Sherri couldn't rest from the effort to make her entry everything that she was capable of. Hour after countless hour poured into her preparations, and other things sometimes slid by, until one day at lunch her father brought her up short.

"Sherri." His quiet tone still managed to reach her in her mental wanderings. "When was the last time you rode Cedar?"

Sherri's thoughts thudded to earth. She thought quickly. "Tuesday." A long pause. "No. Monday." She knew her face was flushed red.

Her father gave her a long, hard stare. "Four days. And he's still in the first ninety-day period of his training."

Sherri stared at her plate. Her appetite was suddenly gone.

"You will be on him this afternoon, without fail." Her dad pointed his fork at her. "Is that clearly understood?"

"Yes, sir."

"And I trust that a four-day lapse will never occur again. That horse is worth too much money to expend on your daydreaming."

Sherri's face burned as she made a pretense of finishing her lunch. She longed to get up and leave, but of course she couldn't until the rest of the family was finished. Only dimly was she aware of what they were now discussing.

"Terry and Shane," her father continued to pass out instructions for the rest of the day. "I want you guys to get that herd up from the south pasture. And then get that bull, #668, into an isolation pen. I'm going to put a little thought on what we're going to do with him."

"He's just plain bloodthirsty," Terry said with concern. "I wish we could get rid of him."

"He's one of only two bulls that we have from the Newton strain, though." The response was thoughtful. "And they cost more than we can afford to put into another one right now."

"So, let somebody else pay for the privilege," Terry grumbled. "He's not worth my neck."

"Well, we'll see." Their father took a last swallow of water. "But as long as he's in the barn area—Tim and Todd, I don't want you anywhere near the cattle pens for any reason. Understood?" Two little heads nodded.

Finally, Sherri was able to escape from the table. Once outside and on the young gelding, her spirits quickly lifted. Actually, she thought, it's been a long time since I've been in trouble with Dad over something like that. It used to happen a lot more than it does now. A half-smile twisted her face as she recognized another stepmother-influence. What things can happen without your even realizing it!

Sherri took Cedar out along the southwest boundary of the ranch in order to be a good long way from the incoming herd. Cedar had been started working on cattle, but a bad-tempered bull was more than she would want to risk him on, just yet.

He was, however, Sherri thought, going to be a nice horse. A full belly of slack hung in the reins as the liver-colored gelding held an easy lope across the crest of the hill. "Maybe I'll have to talk Dad into keeping you, Cedar." She straightened back in her saddle and lifted the reins slightly, without tightening them.

Cedar obligingly ground to a quick halt. Sherri looked down the slope to the ranch driveway that ran along the bottom. Across the field on the opposite side, she could see Shane and Terry moving the herd up from the south pasture. She shook her head as she picked out the rambunctious form of #668. A faint bellow reached her ear, followed by the crack of a bullwhip. The herd was swinging in the general direction of the stock pens by the main barn.

"I wonder if I should go lend a hand?" Sherri mused aloud. "I would if I was on any horse but you. Nothing personal, guy. It's just that I don't know for sure how you'd react to a crew of rowdies like that. You're pretty fresh from school—what do they think they're doing?"

Sherri had been watching the ranch truck roll along the driveway toward the highway as she spoke, but hadn't been paying much attention, assuming that it was her father or Luke. Now, the truck pulled to a stop by the blackberry bushes that clustered along the fence line. Sherri watched as Lynn, Kathleen, Todd, and Timmy piled out and descended on the blackberries, dishes in hand.

"Oh, well." Sherri shrugged. "Dad would probably run them out of there till that herd's gone but I guess they're far enough away—"

She broke off as she saw Lynn gesturing toward the pasture. Todd and Tim skimmed under the fence and took off diagonally across the pasture. It took her a couple of heartbeats to realize that Lynn was sending them to the bushes that ran along the road. It was a couple of hundred yards from where they were.

Was Lynn crazy? Even as the thought came, Sherri realized that her stepmother probably couldn't see the herd from where she was. She was below eye-level of the hill.

"Hey! Hey, you guys!" Even to herself, her shout sounded weak and thin, lacking the power to carry the quarter mile from where she was to the little group by the fence. Terror took hold of her as she saw the bull bellowing and cavorting along the near side of the herd. When they came over the rise, there was going to be trouble. And Terry and Shane were both on the far side of the herd, certain that the bunch would try a last break for freedom in the opposite direction toward the range.

"Lynn!!" The scream tore from Sherri's throat. "Lynn! Todd! No!" She stuck her fingers in her mouth and let loose an ear-splitting whistle. That drew Lynn and Kathleen's attention. Sherri waved frantically, gesturing toward the herd. They waved cheerfully in her direction and turned back to their berries.

"Oh, dear God, make them understand!" Sherri felt panic welling up. "I can't get there in time!" Or could she? In the same second the thought struck, she rammed both heels into her mount's sides, sending Cedar charging down the slope. "Come on, go! Go!" she yelled at him, swiftly increasing his speed to a dead run. She did her best not to think what would happen if he lost his balance at that speed and fell on the uneven slope. The gelding seemed to sense the urgency, responding with all the sprinting power for which his breed was famous. Down the slope and across the field they came, bearing down on the gravel driveway at a speed above forty miles an hour.

Sherri saw Lynn and Kathleen's heads jerk around as the staccato thunder of his hoof beats registered with them. "Hiyah! Cedar! Go! Yah!" Sherri was standing in her stirrups, whaling the driving gelding with the long ends of the reins. "Get up!" There was no time to stop and open the gate. She had to try to force him over it.

"Get up!" She was riding for everything she was worth. She saw Lynn and Kathleen leap back and whirl away as the spraying gravel struck them. She heard one of them cry out in what sounded like anger, but her entire concentration was on Cedar. She felt his muscles bunch as though he would refuse the gate.

Sherri pounded him with her heels and struck him several more times on the shoulders with the reins. His ears went back and he squealed like a bronc, but he gathered himself and soared over the low gate.

"Todd! Timmy!" Sherri shrieked at them. "Get out of here! Get out!"

At that moment, the herd broke over the hill. They were no more than two hundred yards from Sherri, with the boys about halfway between. In the blink of an eye, the black bull gave a strangled bellow and charged.

Todd and Tim dropped their dishes and ran, Tim toward the gate and Todd toward the road. Sherri was yanking at the coiled stock whip that was fastened to the back of her saddle. It came loose, and somehow she managed to get the thong around her wrist and grasp the handle.

Cedar continued to follow her guiding hand. He cut across Tim's backtrack toward the bull. "Hey! Get out of here!" Sherri swung the whip, making it whistle through the air. But she lacked the strength to crack it as her brothers did. And she hadn't counted on its effect on Cedar. With a snort of panic, the young gelding shied away from the whip. Sherri nearly lost her seat as the saddle horn stabbed her in the stomach.

"Whoa! Cedar! Easy!" Sherri tried to regain control; then the bull was there. All in an instant, he was coming at Cedar broadside. Sherri could hear his bellowing ringing in her ears, and she could smell the sweaty stench that clung to him.

"Hey!" She dragged Cedar into a side-spin and struck the bull in the face with the lash as hard as she could. He roared again, doing a plunge that brought him around after them again. Cedar's tail was still toward the monster, and he made use of his natural weapons. With another angry bronc-squeal, he drove both hind feet into the bull's face, jolting Sherri against the front of the saddle again. She heard the thudding smack, followed by a grunt from the bull.

She checked Cedar, spun him around again, and followed up with another whip-slash. Then again and again she struck. Fortunately, it seemed as though Cedar was now more concerned with the bull than with the whip. In a frenzy of panic she wheeled the gelding in a half-circle as the bull backed away. He seemed partially blinded or stunned. Maybe Cedar had kicked him in the eye.

Sherri's throat hurt from yelling, her arm was numb, and her legs trembled from the strain of staying with Cedar's terrified lunging. Then the straying end of the lash flicked the gelding in the flank. With a bawl of his own, he plunged away from the bull. Several half-bucks came near to unseating Sherri. She was trying to haul him around again when the bull apparently spotted Tim racing for the gate. The huge animal bellowed and charged, but even as he did, Sherri could see that Tim was close enough to make it.

Sinking her heels in, Sherri encouraged Cedar to continue his flight in the other direction. Todd was still in the pasture, fleeing toward the far fence and the road. Sherri was surprised he was still there. It seemed like the skirmish with the bull had lasted an hour, but in reality, she knew it had been only a few seconds. It wasn't but another few before she was bearing down on her little brother.

"Todd! Stop!" Sherri gasped. He heard her and reversed his direction. She pulled Cedar up, but the gelding was thoroughly spooked. He wouldn't stand still for her to get a grasp on Todd's arm and yank him up.

"Whoa! Whoa! Easy!" Sherri saw the bull turn from the gate and give his attention back to them. Giving up, she reached out, grasped Cedar's bridle and dropped to the ground. "Get over here!" She grabbed Todd by the back of his belt as he came near, and with strength she'd never known she had, all but threw him into the saddle.

That was the final straw for the much-abused, much-confused Cedar. He shied violently, rearing, and yanking Sherri clear off her feet. The weight of her grip on the bridle tore it half from his head. The gelding's wild plunging and fighting to get free did the rest. In the blink of an eye, Sherri was holding a half of a broken bridle in her hand while Cedar thundered straight up the pasture toward the barn, Todd still on board.

Sherri dropped the bridle and clenched the whip. The roaring bellows of the bull filled her entire mind. She faced him until he was a few feet away, struck blindly at him with the whip, and ran to the side. The acrid stench of the animal struck her just before his shoulder did. The impact threw her fifteen feet away. She landed rolling, came onto her feet, and kept running. In that moment, Sherri was sure that she was going to die. She knew she wouldn't be able to evade the next charge.

Then shouts registered in her mind. From the corner of her eye, she saw Terry bearing down on the bull, cutting it off from her, much as she had from Todd and Tim. The only difference was that his horse was a seasoned cow horse, and he had the strength she lacked to make the bull whip effective.

"Get out, you ugly—" Terry's shout was nearly drowned out by the repeated crack of the whip.

"Sherri!" Another shout came from behind her. That was Shane. His big gelding was flying toward her. He waved his left arm. She understood. Turning to face him, she moved to the left side of his horse. As Shane approached, he slowed slightly. Sherri grabbed the saddle horn and did a cartwheeling leap, as she would have in an Indian-pickup speed contest. She felt Shane's hand clamp on her arm, then she was up.

The ground flashed beneath her; then came a lurch as they cleared the gate. Sherri clung tightly to her brother, not trusting her own balance. He swung a boot over his horse's head and dropped to the ground. The world spun around Sherri as he pulled her down too. She was just aware enough to realize that Shane's face was black with anger.

"What were those dumb fool kids doing in there? Never mind! That's it! That is it!" Three running steps took him to the driver's door of the ranch truck. Yanking it open, he reached beneath the seat and pulled out the Sharps rifle that always stayed there. He pulled out the gun with one hand and shells with the other and began feeding them into the magazine. He worked the pump lever and cradled the rifle in his arm, grabbing his horse's reins as he did so.

"Shane, don't." Sherri's words were almost a sob. "Dad—"

"Shut up." Flinging the gate open, he swung up and rode back into the field.

Sherri leaned over with her hands on her knees. Her breath was still coming in ragged gasps. She wondered whether all the shimmery blackness around the edges of her vision meant that she was losing her mind or that she was about to pass out.

"Sherri?"

She looked up to see the pasty-white face of her little brother. "Sherri? You okay?" His eyes were wide and tearless, but his voice could barely be heard. "I'm sorry."

Sherri reached out and grabbed the little boy. "It's okay, Timmy. We're all okay." She held him tightly as she heard his small voice again.

"We didn't know they were in there, Sherri. Honest."

"Never mind, Timmy. Nobody's hurt. Don't worry about it now." She felt the shaking start in her legs and move up through her whole body. The abrupt bark of the rifle made her flinch and gasp. The bull's bellowing stopped.

Sherri released Tim when Shane and Terry came back to the gate. The ground was still pitching about beneath her feet, but Sherri managed to stand and lean back against the hood of the pickup. For the first time she looked over at Lynn and Kathleen.

They stood transfixed, eyes wide and faces white, but neither said a word.

Todd came running down from the barn. He stopped next to Tim, out of breath. "I shut the corral gate for Cedar, Sherri, and put the lid over the trough, but he's still pretty excited."

"Okay." Sherri figured Todd would have been able to see most of what had happened.

The gate clicked shut behind her two older brothers. Sherri looked up at them as they led their horses toward the truck. It was hard to tell who was hotter or dirtier, them or the horses. Little rivulets coursed down the horses' sweat-blackened coats in dozens of places. The guys' shirts were damp and their faces streaked.

Shane had absolutely no expression on his face at all as he ejected the shells from the rifle and stowed it beneath the truck seat again. The silence grew larger as Terry pulled off his hat and ran his arm across his face. His glance shifted from one person to the next, all the way around the group.

"All right," he said quietly. "Now I'm going to hear about how a dumb thing like that happened in the first place."

He was looking at Sherri, and she didn't miss the tension in his voice. She just bit her lip and looked down. What could she say without incriminating Lynn or Kathleen?

"What about it, guys?" The volume in Terry's voice was rising as he turned to the boys. "Spit it out!"

"Terry." The rasping sound was scarcely recognizable as Lynn's voice.

He looked at her in surprise.

"It's my fault. I sent them into the pasture." Lynn gulped and took a couple of steps forward. "We were just picking berries, and I wanted them to go over and get the ones on the bushes by the road."

Sherri cringed at the falter in the woman's voice. It didn't sound like her at all. But in spite of how upset she was, Lynn was plainly unwilling that Terry would blame the boys for what had happened.

"They were just doing what I told them to do. I had no idea there was anything in that field or that you guys were driving cattle up there—"

"No idea?" Terry cut her off sharply. "We just finished discussing that blasted bull and this pasture change at lunch! How short is your memory?"

"I'm sorry." Sherri could hear the threat of tears in Lynn's voice.

Terry looked away for a moment, then spun around and dealt the hood of the pickup a sickening blow with his fist. "You're sorry!" He was truly yelling now. "We just had three people nearly killed, and you're sorry! What good is sorry? Look around you! This isn't Milwaukee! Don't—"

"Stop it, Terry!" Sherri startled even herself with her words that came out almost as a scream. "Stop it! Leave her alone!"

He tried to speak, but she gave him no chance. Her words poured out in a torrent. "Do you think she did it on purpose? That really makes a lot of sense, doesn't it? You've got no right to say anything to her anyway! Just leave her alone!" Terry actually took a step back as Sherri advanced on him.

Abruptly she cut herself off, making a wild grab for some semblance of emotional control. She turned away, stumbling a little as the dizziness upset her balance again. Taking a deep breath, she stepped to the door of the truck. "Tim, Todd, into the back. Now!" As the boys scooted for the tailgate, Sherri swung herself through the open door into the driver's seat. Jamming the clutch down, she slammed the door and started the engine. "Are you two riding or walking?" She asked the question without looking out, but both Kathleen and Lynn came around the truck hurriedly and got in.

Sherri swung the truck around and headed toward the main barn. Thick silence filled the cab. Sherri propped her elbow on the open window and leaned her head against her hand. She was feeling the beginnings of a pounding tension headache. No one said anything until the truck halted outside the barn. Sherri sighed and dropped her head against the steering wheel for a moment.

"Sherri? What's going to happen?" The soft question was Kathleen's.

Sherri didn't look up. "I don't know." Another long pause. "But right now, I've got a horse to calm down and cool out." She opened the door and pushed herself out. "See you later."

Automatically, she got a halter from the barn and went through the motions of soothing Cedar. She heard her own voice talking quietly to the excited gelding as she unsaddled him and cleaned him off. Eventually she was able to give him a drink and turn him out with the other horses.

Sherri walked slowly up to the house, skirting it so she could come in the end door. She didn't want to talk to anybody. Making her way into her room, she collapsed into the big rocker. The room still seemed to be turning.

In an attempt to focus her eyes on something, she randomly picked a spot in space, only to find herself staring at her months-old sketch of Blind Valley that leaned against the wall on the middle bookshelf. The memory of the bitterness of that day came swiftly back. Some distant part of herself spoke up: Think how glad you'd have been to have had anything to blame on her that day. Now you're defending her carelessness?

Sherri leaned her head back and blinked at the tears that were forming, transferring her gaze to the ceiling light until it swam into a blur. "Lord," she whispered, "thank You that no one was killed. And please, somehow, let me be half as gracious to her now as she was to me that day." Sherri closed her eyes. Even then, she could feel the dizziness. She felt as though everything were whirling around and around and around. . . .

She must have fallen asleep, for Kathleen woke her from the doorway.

"Sherri?"

Sherri looked up groggily.

"Supper is ready. Your dad called, but I guess you didn't hear."

"Tell him I'm not hungry." Sherri didn't move, other than to rub her eyes.

"Are you all right?" Kathleen came closer, a frown creasing her face.

"Yeah. I'm all right."

"You don't look it. Your shirt's torn, and there's a huge bruise on your arm. I didn't notice it before."

Sherri turned to look at her left shoulder. Sure enough. The sleeve from her shirt was virtually gone, and the entire upper part of her arm was a swollen-looking purplish black. She heard heavy footsteps in the hall and looked up to see her father stride into the room.

"Just wanted to make sure you're okay," he said. "Can you move that arm?" His hand on her shoulder was surprisingly gentle.

She tried moving it. "Yeah, it just hurts a little. Must be where he hit me." Even Sherri realized that her statement didn't sound very intelligent.

"We can talk about it later. Don't you want to come and eat something?" he asked.

"I'm not hungry. But I'm okay."

Sherri felt her eyes closing and wished that they would leave. There was a short pause. "All right. Get some sleep," her father said.

"Hope you feel better," Kathleen murmured.

She listened to their steps fade away, then hoisted herself from the chair. She grabbed her robe and made her way across the hall to the bathroom. The supper table was the least appealing place on earth at the moment. She just couldn't face going over all the details of what had happened—not now.

Besides, she knew Terry was going to have to apologize to Lynn for what he'd said—no, not what, but how. And Sherri didn't know how her dad was going to take the fact that Shane had shot the bull. All in all, she thought that a soak in a hot tub beat sitting through dinner.

By the time she dragged herself back to her room, she felt drugged. She knew it was just exhaustion, but her legs and arms were clumsy and slow. Everything hurt when she rolled into bed. She wished she'd thought to take some aspirin while she was in the bathroom, but it wasn't worth it to have to get back up now.

Sometime in the night, Sherri awoke suddenly, sitting bolt upright in bed. She wasn't even aware that she had cried out, but she realized that she was shaking from head to foot. She couldn't escape the grip of the horrible dream she'd been having: she'd been back in the pasture, on foot, trying to beat the bull in a foot-race to Tim. On and on she went, straining and struggling, but knowing that no matter how hard she tried, the bull was going to get there first.

The door opened and Lynn slipped into the room. "Sherri? Sherri, honey, are you all right?"

Sherri's throat was too tight to let her answer. She still felt the dragging effect of total exhaustion, and that seemed to be taking its toll on her emotions as well. Lynn came to the edge of the bed and sat down. "Bad dreams?"

Sherri nodded.

"I can imagine. I haven't been to sleep yet, myself." Lynn paused, and Sherri could hear the catch of breath in her throat. "I must have lost ten years off my life today when I saw that bull hit you."

Sherri brushed at her eyes with both hands, wondering afresh if Lynn felt any resentment at all for Terry's reaction.

"I appreciate your sticking up for me the way you did today, Sherri. I wouldn't have been surprised if you hadn't, and Terry was right in what he was saying."

"No, he wasn't."

"But—"

"It wasn't your fault." Sherri stared down at the bedspread, barely able to discern its pattern in the darkness. She tried to figure out the words for what she was thinking. "Really. He wasn't right to blame you. Somebody should have made sure that you understood what was being said at lunch today. There are a lot of things here that are different. . . . They can't think that you will automatically know everything about stuff that's all new to you."

Lynn was quiet for several moments, but her next comment brought Sherri's head up in surprise. "I guess it worked that way for both of us, hmm? New things, I mean."

Sherri just stared at her, once again feeling the surprise of her stepmother's perception. Maybe the words and apologies she'd tried so long to think of wouldn't be necessary anyway. Sherri was even more surprised when Lynn reached out for her and held her close.

"It's all right, Sherri. Just relax and go back to sleep."

Sherri wasn't sure why she started crying, but the next moment she was sobbing outright, with Lynn holding her like Sherri had held Timmy that afternoon, stroking her hair and talking quietly. She felt something uncomfortable and hard come loose inside her. I don't need to say it, Sherri thought. She knows anyway; she really does, and it's all right.

Chapter Eighteen

A week later, when school opened again, Sherri still carried a shining welt on the upper part of her arm. It wasn't as sore anymore, and she could move it without pain, but if anyone so much as looked as though he were going to touch it, she felt herself flinch.

She sat on the familiar, chugging school bus and watched the same kids boarding at stop after stop. It seemed a little unreal, and Sherri felt as though she were watching everything from a long distance away. Beside her, Kyle was as quiet as she was. Sherri wondered whether he, also, felt like an awful lot of water had gone under the bridge during the summer. The last week at the ranch had been unusual. To Sherri's surprise—and relief—her father hadn't said any more to her about the incident. Kyle had recounted the dinner conversation to her, and she had been amazed at how low-key everything had been.

There had been a brief apology from Terry, without so much as a comment from their father. All he'd said was that they were undoubtedly better off without #668, and would everybody please be more careful in the future. Wonders never cease, Sherri thought in amazement. I'd love to know what Lynn says to him about these things when we're not around.

Possibly, she wondered, Dad might just have been trying to keep things pleasant for Shane's last few days at home. Sherri already missed her brother more than she would have admitted to anyone. He was off to college—on the other side of the country. They wouldn't be seeing him until Christmas.

The real shocker was discovering a definite gap when Kathleen also returned to fall classes. Get a grip, Sherri! she'd told herself. But the recent, budding camaraderie with her stepsister insisted on leaving a small void where she'd hardly expected one. She sighed slightly, wondering whether the rest of her life was going to be one long series of unsettling changes.

I'm trying to remember to watch for Your hand in the changes, Lord, Sherri prayed silently as she watched the familiar, red-brick school building appear in her window. But it's not the easiest thing I've ever tried to do.

At least school itself hadn't seemed to change much. The same familiar sounds and smells struck Sherri as she settled into a seat in her homeroom: paper, chalk dust, clanging locker doors, and the tinny jangle of the bell.

Sherri didn't miss Karen's double take when her friend first walked into the room and spotted her. Karen's comment when she found a seat nearby was scarcely less revealing. "Well, you must have had an eventful summer," she remarked as she surveyed Sherri from head to foot.

There was no time for talk, though. The students gradually fell quiet as their homeroom instructor began the familiar announcements.

We're juniors, Sherri thought, feeling a strange tingle. Next year at this time, it will be my last year! For the moment she was too preoccupied with the thought itself to remember how differently she'd felt about that when she'd sat through Shane's graduation.

Sherri kept one ear on the announcements while she looked around. As long as she was acknowledging change, she had to include many of her classmates. She was surprised in the differences—even since a few months ago when school let out. Well, she admitted, things changed for me too, so why not for them?

Suddenly her full attention snapped back to what Mr. Tedd, the homeroom advisor, was saying. An all-school project. A special fund raiser for the new gymnasium. . . . The school was going to hold a Rodgers and Hammerstein production around Thanksgiving.

"This is going to be in addition to the regular Christmas concert and program," Mr. Tedd was saying. "So we're all going to have to pitch in and help." A few groans greeted that announcement, but he went on. "There will be tryouts, and all the usual sort of thing, of course. But this morning the principal would like me to collect the names of anyone who would be willing to help with publicity and ticket sales and things like that."

No one was more surprised than Sherri when she heard her own voice. She didn't even remember putting up her hand. "I think I might be able to help with some photos and fliers and things."

There was a brief pause. Mr. Tedd looked at her as though she'd just shot up through the floorboards. "Ah, sure, Sherri. That would be great." He nodded to Mrs. Holmes, who scribbled busily on her pad. Sherri settled back in her seat, trying to ignore the sidelong looks from some of her classmates. She felt a slight flush on her cheeks. Are they that surprised? she thought.

Before the week was over, Sherri found herself in an after-school meeting with Mr. King, one of the English teachers who was also the yearbook advisor, and a handful of other students, most of whom she didn't know.

They'd all volunteered to help with publicity for the production. Sherri was beginning to feel a little uncomfortable as she noticed that most of them seemed to know each other. The few that she did recognize were seniors. Probably, she thought, they've all worked on this kind of stuff before so much. . . . What did I think I was doing, anyway?

Sherri sat quietly, not adding anything to the discussion. They were talking about making posters and finding places to put them up.

"We have to come up with something sharp this time," said one of the girls that Sherri knew. Her name was Marsha. "Not like last year for the ice carnival when we wound up drawing them out by hand."

That drew a general laugh from the others.

"They are thinking about the possibility of having some photos done," Mr. King remarked. "If they do, we might be able to come up with something from that."

Sherri's heart leaped. She started to speak and her mouth went dry. Little hands reached up and grabbed her throat. Say it, you fool, she ordered herself. With an actual physical effort, Sherri forced a word out. "Sir?"

Mr. King's attention jerked to her as though he'd just noticed her. "Yes? Wait, I'm sorry. I'm not sure I remember your name." He shuffled through his papers, looking for the list.

"Sherri James, sir." Sherri thought her voice sounded nearly an octave higher than normal.

"Oh, yes. Of course!" He looked at her again with an added degree of surprise. "That's what it is. I've been sitting here trying to figure out whom you reminded me of. I should have realized that you were one of Paul and Debbie's kids. I went to school here with your mother—you look exactly like her."

That threw Sherri's scant composure to the corners of the room. "Oh. I, um. Oh." Pull yourself together, nut, she thought.

"Yes, go ahead, Sherri. I'm sorry. I just threw that in for free."

The other students chuckled.

"I was thinking . . . well when you mentioned the photos, I was wondering if they had anyone in mind yet to do them or to do the processing and printing."

"Ah, well." He thought for a moment. "I'm really not sure. Why?"

"If they were planning on paying an agency or a freelancer, or something, I was thinking that I might be able to save you—save us—some money, and then possibly, if those funds are already designated for the play, that some of the money could be used for getting some real nice posters actually printed, using some of the photos." Sherri wasn't finished, but she had to pause to gulp for breath and steady her voice. That was the longest speech she'd ever made aloud in school.

Mr. King looked skeptical. "How would you manage that?"

"I can get supplies and do processing at wholesale cost where I work. And there's camera equipment that I can use. Plus, I can get typesetting things done there and work on layouts and stuff for personal projects. So, in the school's case, all they would have to pay for would be the cost of the film and paper and the actual printing cost for the posters."

There was a fairly long silence. Sherri thought she was actually starting to get used to being stared at. She tried to exhale without letting it sound as loud and shaky as it felt. She was surprised to realize that she was actually perspiring.

"Where do you work, Sherri?" Mr. King's voice was puzzled.

"At the Krayfor Agency."

"Seriously?" The man's eyebrows drew together.

Sherri saw a couple of students glance up in surprise. She just nodded. The skeptical look hadn't quite left Mr. King's face. "You realize that some of the things they would want done with the photos might be a little involved?"

"Um-hmm." Sherri nodded again, feeling her face flush. But, sensing that he was about to object, she rushed on, hardly believing what she was doing. "I've done some similar things, if you'd like to look at them before you say anything to anyone. Black & white and color. Blowups and everything. Plus, I can do the PMTs for the posters. It really wouldn't

179

be very expensive at all. Probably, even including the cost of the poster printing, it wouldn't be much more than half of what they'd spend on a agency or a freelancer to do the photos alone."

A long discussion had followed. Sherri had called Mrs. Vey and explained the situation, telling her that she would be late for work, but as it was, she didn't get to Krayfor until barely an hour before closing time.

For the first time she could remember in her school years, Sherri felt as though she had at least one foot on solid ground with some other students. She'd spent an hour or more hunched over a desk, busily sketching trial layouts and explaining until her throat was dry. Their knowledge of layouts and artwork was far more extensive than hers had been just a short while ago, and she could see that several of them were still miles ahead of her, but none of them seemed to know much about the pricing and how different printing effects related to cost.

One of the girls, Tara, whom Sherri hadn't known before, struck up a conversation with her as the meeting finally ended and they made their way outside. "It was nice to have you here, Sherri. I've seen you around a lot, but I never thought you had anything to do with stuff like—well, I mean, you just never seemed interested—I—" Tara fumbled around and stopped, obviously embarrassed at her own thoughtlessness.

"Things have changed a little for me these past few months." Sherri spoke the words with a calmness that she didn't feel, trying to visualize how Lynn would have responded to a comment like that. "I guess what feels like being shy to yourself can seem like something totally different to others."

"You shy?" Tara rolled her eyes. "You'd have a hard time convincing a lot of others about that."

Sherri was trying to figure out how to answer that, when Tara apparently decided to switch to a safer topic. "How did you ever get a job at Krayfor, anyway?"

Sherri smiled, and her answer seemed to leap out of its own volition. "It was a special gift from the Lord, Tara. I had nothing to do with how it happened."

"It what?" Tara actually stopped and stood in the middle of the hallway. She looked down at the floor rather than up, but Sherri could see the amused expression anyway. The other girl was trying not to laugh. Sherri fought the surge of embarrassment.

Now why did I say that, Sherri thought. I've made more potential friends in the last hour than I have in the last five years. Why complicate things?

Because you said the truth, Sherri, the small voice in her mind broke into her thought. Answer her. She really wants to know.

She hesitated, then plunged ahead. "A gift from God. I mean it." Sherri forced a smile to a face that didn't really feel like smiling. "I've always wanted to be involved in artwork and production, but I never had much of a chance. Last spring my dad remarried, and my stepmother put me in contact with Mrs. Vey at Krayfor, who offered me the job before I really knew what was going on."

"So why is that a—um—a gift?"

"I know that the Lord controls the circumstances around us and that He works things out how they'd be best for His children. I know He's given me a chance to get a head start on my college training, and that's a special gift to me."

Tara finally looked up. Her expression wasn't amused anymore. It was wary. "That's the craziest thing I've ever heard."

That was hard to take. Sherri knew the flush was creeping up her face again. "I guess a lot of people think that, Tara." Sherri bit her lip. "But I know it's right; sometimes I wish I was better about making people understand why. Do you even know what I mean when I talk about 'God's children'?"

"Yeah. Isn't everyone?" Tara turned away with a shrug and continued down the hall toward the end doors. "All from Adam and Eve, or whatever."

"No," Sherri tried to keep pace with her without seeming to scramble. "Everyone isn't. That's what I mean."

"Look, I have to scoot, okay?" Tara almost interrupted her. "It was nice meeting you and all, Sherri. I guess I'll be seeing you around."

"Okay." Sherri had no chance to say more than that before Tara hurried down the steps away from her. She looked after the other girl and sighed, gripping her books a little more tightly. "Craziest thing she ever heard. Great." Sherri muttered as she started toward Lynn's car. "Real smooth, Sherri."

The preaching of the cross is to them that perish foolishness.

"I know, Lord," Sherri said inwardly. "I want to do what's right. Really I do. But why do I always come out of a situation like that feeling like such an idiot?" But even as she reached for the car's ignition, the obvious answer rose up and stared her in the face. You've never been in a "situation like that" before, honesty forced her to admit. Not once in your life!

Sherri remembered Tara's amazement. She'd never before had a clue as to why, by her standards, Sherri seemed so out of touch.

You've spent your whole school life feeling like an idiot, Sherri told herself, but you've never spoken up enough even to let others understand why—whether they agree or not!

"Is that why you gave me the job, Lord? To get me to speak out?" She asked the question aloud this time. She stared at a spot on the windshield for a few more moments before she turned the engine on and backed out of her parking slot. Pausing, she opened the tape cassette holder, rummaged around, then popped a tape into the player and began to hum softly with the words of the song as she drove away. "Come, Lord, take me by the hand; come, Lord, teach a child to stand. Show me where to go, and tell me what to say; Give Thy Word to light my path and point the way. . . . "

"Speak Lord" © 1980 by Nicky Chavers. Used with permission.

Chapter Nineteen

Mrs. Vey was pleased to hear about Sherri's upcoming contribution to the school project. She even promised her help if it was needed, saying that she would try to arrange to get the school a good deal on the printing costs, if that's what they decided to do. Sherri's thoughts were full all that afternoon and evening. So much happens so fast, she thought.

But during the next few weeks, Sherri had no time to think about anything. She had until the fifteenth of September to get her photo entries finished for the Kiston show. Work with the publicity for the school project was already underway, calling for after-school time once or twice a week, but she didn't dare neglect Cedar's training. Schoolwork was something else this year, too! She was getting an introduction to a ghastly subject called physics. That, on top of Algebra II and third-year French, was going to be the end of her, Sherri was certain.

From the time she crawled out of bed every morning at five o'clock to the time she fell back into it around ten or eleven at night, Sherri's whole life moved on split-second timing. Even with all she had to do, her father would tolerate no slack in her work around home. Sherri hung on to the approaching deadline on the fifteenth as though it were a life preserver. Surely things would ease up a little then! Right now, the photography show stayed at the front of her mind with an urgency that pressed almost enough to hurt. She postponed projects and scrimped on time wherever she could in order to have a few extra minutes to spend in the darkroom. Never had she labored this much over the tiniest details of exposure and framing. Never had she pored over magazine and book photography articles with such intensity.

Mrs. Vey frequently took time away from whatever she was doing to keep track of how Sherri's entries were coming along. She offered suggestions from time to time and, like the other Krayfor employees, did her best to keep up with Sherri's running flow of questions. Especially when the time came to mat and frame the finished photos, she was a goldmine of honest, professional feedback.

But Sherri was her own greatest critic, scrutinizing frames and mats to the last detail. Time after time, she would pull a finished piece apart and start all over. The dark frame would look better over here, with the blue mat, she thought. Again and again she rearranged the photos in a mock set-up of the space that Mrs. Vey had told her she would have available. But finally, on the night of the fourteenth, she was actually finished. She'd told her dad that she would probably be late, and had received special permission to miss supper and stay as late into the evening as she needed. The only stipulation was that she call before she started home.

Now, it was nearly ten o'clock. Sherri stood, rumpled and disheveled, in the midst of her finished display. Her sense of perspective was gone as she stared numbly at the frames surrounding her. Two days ago she'd looked at them and been pleased. The personality of the Rockview Ranch came through strongly, she felt. But now. . . .

"Are you about finished, Sherri?" Mrs. Vey came out of her office. "If you want me to help you package them, we need to get started."

"Yes. I guess I'm as finished as I'm ever going to be." Sherri brushed a grimy hand across her face.

"I think you've done a good job." Mrs. Vey came past her to scrutinize the frame of one shot. "Are you pleased?"

"I don't know. Yesterday I was. Tonight, I'm just so tired. I don't know. I've lost my critical sense, I think."

"It's time to quit, then," Mrs. Vey said with finality. "You won't help another thing by fussing with it when you feel that way."

"All right. Where do we start?" Sherri began clearing away the last of the framing tools. A little over an hour later, she was finally on her way home.

I am going to be dead in school tomorrow, she thought. But tomorrow night, I can go home and get some extra rest! Come what may, those things are finished! She heaved a sigh of relief.

She'd thought that the three weeks until the show results were announced would take forever to pass. She was pleasantly surprised, however. There was a backlog of things that she had to catch up on, so there wasn't a lot of time to sit around and wonder about anything.

A couple of weekends later, Sherri had dedicated an entire Saturday afternoon to some roping lessons for Cedar. The beautiful gelding was turning out to be a born cow horse. Her father was so pleased with him that Sherri knew Cedar would wind up as a permanent fixture at Rockview. Cedar still had a long way to go with the roping business, though. A horse could be a wonder with cutting, driving, and everything else and still be worthless when it came to roping stock from his back.

Just barely, Cedar was beginning to get the idea to back away from the pull on the rope, instead of giving in to it. But he had a tendency to want to turn to the side as he backed away, and that put the pressure on the saddle at the wrong—and weakest—angle. Again and again Sherri corrected him, with pats and praises when he did it right. Cedar would blow noisily through his nose and try again. He was a patient soul and wanted to please—whatever in the world she was trying to get him to do!

The fall weather was sunny and clear. Mild days like this were numbered, Sherri knew. Already, the fiery-gold colors of autumn covered the mountainsides and the trees along the pasture. The glow of the aspens and the tan of the grass were reminders of the winter cold that was only a few weeks away. The snowy caps on the peaks were noticeably larger, and the evenings brought chill winds and plummeting temperatures.

When Sherri finally decided that Cedar had had enough, she turned him toward the alleyway to the barn. She was surprised to see Lynn sitting on the top rail of the adjoining corral. "Hi, what are you doing there?"

"Just watching. I didn't want to interrupt you."

"Well, he's coming along, I guess. But he's been having a hard time getting the hang of the rope."

"No puns intended?" Lynn's smile came quickly.

"What? Oh, no! I mean—" Sherri shook her head and rolled her eyes.

"Sorry. Bad joke, I know. He's beautiful, though. Do you suppose we'll keep him?"

"I don't know for sure." Sherri dismounted as she came near. "I think so. I think Dad wanted to from the time he first saw him. But he never likes to tell us until the last minute, in case he changes his mind or gets a really good offer for him."

"He thinks that if he changes his mind, you or one of the others will pester him to keep Cedar?"

"Partly, I guess." Sherri smiled wryly. "But I think it's more that he doesn't want us to know he's as attached to the animals as we are."

That brought a laugh from Lynn as she followed Sherri into the barn and watched her put Cedar up. Talk turned to some of the other young horses that they'd brought home from the auction the previous spring. Sherri brought her up to date on the marvelous little sorrel, the big brown gelding with the Olympic-class sprint that her father figured would bring top price as a bulldogging horse, and the stumblefoot bay that everyone wished they'd left at the auction.

"He sounds about my speed," Lynn said. "Maybe you'd better leave him here for me."

"Get serious!" Sherri objected. "You've really come a long way this summer. You actually ride now—like a rider, that is, not like a dude." She slipped Cedar's halter off. Closing the door of the stall, she turned back to Lynn. "Now all you need is to get proficient with a rope, and you'll be all set."

"What a laugh!" Lynn's voice rose in protest. "I picked one of those things up once, and it felt like cable wire. How you ever do anything with those glorified pieces of iron, I'll never know."

"No, no, no. They're not that bad! They have to be stiff or they won't hold a loop. Come out here for a minute. Let me show you." Sherri seized Lynn by the arm and propelled her back to the corral, pulling a couple of lariats off the aisle wall as she went.

Once back in the corral, she gave one to Lynn and showed her how to hold the base of the loop so that the rope could run through her fingers to increase or decrease the size of the loop, and what to do with the rest of the rope.

"Now when you're aiming at something, you can't forget about the hold you have with the other hand." Sherri ducked as Lynn attempted to whirl the loop around her head. "You can have your loop exactly right and the throw exactly right, but if your loop has twenty feet to cover and you give it only ten feet of rope to travel on, you're not doing anybody much good."

Again and again, Lynn tried to follow Sherri's example of flipping the loop over a fence post, but things didn't seem to be progressing very well. Twice she hit herself in the head with the rope, and once she managed to settle the noose around Sherri, but she came nowhere near to the post. Soon both of them were nearly doubled over in helpless laughter.

"What is going on out here?" Sherri's father came through the door from the barn. "I can hear you two all the way from the back feedlot."

Fresh giggles greeted him as Lynn tried to untwist the lariat from her latest attempt. "Honey, I don't think this is as easy as it looks," she said with a faint note of exasperation. "The dumb thing goes everywhere but where it's supposed to."

"What made you decide to try?" He stepped over to her and took the snarled lariat.

"I don't really know." Lynn hadn't quite stopped laughing. "I guess we're just creatively wasting time."

Sherri's father didn't comment as he looked from his wife to his daughter. Sherri caught the twitch of a smile at the corner of his mouth. It distracted her enough so that she didn't see the almost imperceptible movement of his arm until it was too late. Swift as a striking rattler, the rope in his hands shot out toward Sherri and circled her just above the elbows.

"Hey!" she exclaimed, pulling back. But it did her no good. With a single, practiced yank, her father brought her across the corral. Another jerk and a twist, and Sherri came spinning into the halfhitch that seemed to form by itself, binding her hands firmly to her sides.

"Now that's what these ropes are good for." He pulled his wife backwards into his arms. "Putting troublemaking daughters where they belong for a little while." He held Lynn when she would have helped Sherri, and he joined their chuckles as Sherri struggled out of the rope.

"So how's that gelding coming along?" her father asked as Sherri was finally coiling up both lariats.

"Okay. He's fine with everything but the roping, and he's coming around with that."

"Do you think you're going to keep him, honey?" Lynn asked.

"Don't rightly know yet." Her husband took off his hat and pushed his fingers through his hair. "Cheller is going to foal in the spring. We might need another good stock horse around. But it's a little early to say for sure."

"He's just so beautiful. Unusual, I guess. Or at least I haven't seen many others like him since I've been here. And he's so sweet tempered."

"Yes, he's striking," Sherri's father admitted, reaching into the tack room to flick off the light and close the door. "But you're starting to sound just like Sherri and the boys. They get themselves all attached to these horses when they're strictly for business and ranching purposes." Unconsciously, he gave his own gray gelding a pat on the nose as they passed its stall.

Lynn and Sherri exchanged glances and started laughing all over again. He stopped and looked at the pair of them. "What?" he asked.

Neither was about to answer, so Sherri quickly changed the subject to something that needed to be talked about anyway.

"Hey, you guys?"

"Hey, what?" her dad asked.

"I have a friend coming with me to the services tomorrow. Is it okay if we pick her up?" The question was a formality, Sherri knew. Her dad had always made it clear that he'd drive any distance out of the way for such a reason.

"Absolutely." His response was typical. "What's her name?"

"Tara. She's a year ahead of me in school. I just met her this fall."

"Do you want to bring her back here for dinner?" Lynn asked.

Sherri grinned. "I was hoping you'd offer. I'd like to— but I didn't ask her. And she might say no. It was hard enough to get her to agree to church."

"Well, make it sound appealing." Her dad suggested. "What are we having? Are we grilling something?"

"Do fish swim in the sea?" Lynn smiled. "The steaks are already out of the freezer."

"Great. If she won't come this time, we'll get her here another time. Sherri, maybe we can—" The shrill, double-beep of the intercom on the telephone cut him off. He turned back to the phone that hung on the wall by the tack room and picked up the receiver. "Yeah? . . . Who? . . . Oh. Yeah, she's done. . . right here. Just a second." He held the receiver out to Sherri. "For you. It's your boss."

"Hello?" Sherri stuck her other hand into her pocket to warm the fingers that were feeling a bit chilled. "Oh really? I didn't know that. . . . Well, um, I guess I don't know why not. . . . I'll have to check with Dad. . . . Oh. Okay. Well, okay. Just a second. I'll ask them."

Sherri turned to face her dad and her stepmother with a slightly puzzled expression. "Mrs. Vey wants me to go to an exhibit with her this coming Monday evening."

He began to nod his consent, but Sherri went on. "She'd like for you two to come, if you possibly can. She says she thinks it would be good for us to be there together. But it's all the way over in Centerville." Sherri was already anticipating a negative response when her father looked at Lynn with a question in his eyes.

She answered simply, "Why not?"

"Okay. Tell her we'll all be there. Just get good directions." Sherri's father pulled a pencil from his pocket and handed it to her.

Sherri turned back to the phone in surprise and repeated their verdict. She was tied up for several minutes, getting directions and times and several other details. When she finally hung up, only her father was still in the barn.

"We're supposed to be there at seven. And I guess it's sort of formal."

"Okay. Why don't you run through those directions with me while they're still fresh in your mind." He reached out to take the sheet from her. "Oh, wait." He looked at her scribbling. "That's Renner Hall. I know where that is."

"You do?" Sherri was skeptical.

"Sure." His smile twisted a little. "I used to go there a lot with your mom."

"Oh." Sherri stuffed her hands deeper into her pockets and looked out the front door of the barn.

"She used to like to go over there every time there was an art exhibit or a special show. We went to a concert there just a couple weeks before Timmy was born." Sherri heard her father's slight sigh. "I suppose that's farther back than you can really remember very well."

Sherri just nodded. Desperately she tried to think of something to say. "We're going to be doing a musical at school around Thanksgiving. Did I tell you that yet?" she asked, though she knew full well that she hadn't.

"No." There was a rather long pause. "Well, maybe we'll have to make it a family event to go."

Sherri clenched her hands into fists. Summoning her courage, she swung around to face him again, pushing a smile into place. "You better plan on it. I'm on the publicity committee—that's how I met Tara. If you won't buy tickets, I'll disown you all."

"You are? On the committee, I mean? Really?" Her father seemed truly surprised.

"Um-hmm. I might even be taking the pictures. Anyway, I'm trying to figure out how to get them some good promotional posters printed at the miser's budget they have."

His face grew thoughtful. "You really enjoy this stuff, don't you, Sherri?"

She just bit her lip and nodded.

"I asked you once before, but I didn't get much of an answer. Is this what you want to take up in college?"

Sherri glanced at him quickly, then away, then back again before she made herself say the single syllable. "Yes."

"Why is it so hard to say so, Sherri?" Her father fixed her with a puzzled stare. "Do you think I'm going to object? I don't. And I know your mom would have approved. It would have delighted her."

"I know." Sherri walked a few steps away to adjust a halter and lead rope on their peg. "Or at least I guess I knew that." The hands retreated into their pockets again. She took another few steps, then faced her father again. "I guess it's just hard to say out loud."

He tilted his head inquiringly, still not understanding her reasoning.

"I want to do it so much." The words suddenly poured out in a rush. "But I've never known if I was going to be able to, or if I was going to be talented enough, or if I could make it through a college art or photography program. And if I didn't say anything, then if I couldn't do it nobody would know how much I'd wanted to, and it would be easier for me to pretend that it didn't matter." Sherri knew that the topsy-turvy string of words probably wasn't making much sense. She gritted her teeth against the urge to withdraw and clam up. "But I've been learning a little, I guess, about how the Lord can use your interests to open up doors for you; so I guess now I'm just waiting to see what's going to happen."

Her father was quiet for a long time. The afternoon sunbeams slanted into the barn. Fall evenings were coming more quickly.

"Sherri, I don't think I've fully realized, until this year, what an extra strain it put on you to grow up in this kind of situation as the only girl."

Sherri smiled a little, for lack of having anything to say. What kind of response did he expect her to make to that?

"But I know that I'm thankful to God for the things that I see coming out in you now."

Sherri looked away, embarrassed.

"And I thank the Lord, also, for bringing someone really special to us, who helped straighten out a lot of things."

Sherri heard the question in his voice, though he hadn't really asked her anything. She let loose a silent breath before meeting her father's eyes. "Me too," she said quietly.

Chapter Twenty

Mrs. Vey met them in the lobby as she'd promised. Sherri responded rather mechanically to her boss's greeting. Her attention was fastened on the cathedral-ceilinged lobby with its cushioned carpeting, chandeliers, and expensive paintings.

"So what kind of a show is this, exactly?" Sherri was a little awed by the atmosphere. "This is sure different from the last one we were at."

"Yes, it is different."

Something in Mrs. Vey's tone brought Sherri's attention back to earth. There was a tension, or excitement, there.

Seeing Sherri's slight frown, Mrs. Vey smiled. "Sherri, this is the semiannual exhibit for the Northwestern Photographers Association. They're a society made up mostly, but not entirely, of professionals."

"Professional—meaning they contract?" Sherri did a quick review of the terms she'd learned during the summer.

"Contract photographers, staff photographers, and freelancers. Plus a few serious 'hobbyists.' "

Listening to that last sentence, Sherri became aware that Mrs. Vey wasn't the only one smiling. Her confusion grew as she realized that her father and Lynn were both wearing broad, excited grins.

EVERY PERFECT GIFT

"Sherri." Mrs. Vey seemed a little nonplused, but still pleased. "With your parents' permission, I took a few liberties with the setup that you did—or thought you did—for the Kiston show. Here." She seemed to switch trains of thought suddenly. "I'd like you to take a quick look at this. It's the judging results for this NPA exhibit."

Sherri took the sheet of stiff parchment that was thrust into her hand. With a last puzzled glance at her boss, Sherri turned her attention to the list of names: Best of Show, Best Theme, Best Single, Runner Up, Third Place. . . . A long list of unfamiliar names ran two thirds of the way down the page. Then, near the bottom, Sherri saw her own name leap off the paper. She blinked, then read it again.

Five entries were listed under the category "Honorable Mention: Theme Exhibits." Among them, "Sheryl Renee James: ROCKVIEW MOODS."

Sherri stared at the paper, feeling the room contract and pulse around her. All of the conversations seemed to buzz to a louder pitch, then fade far away. "I'm not sure I understand." Sherri barely heard her own whisper. The sound of her father's voice was reassuring.

"Mrs. Vey thought that your work had a good chance in a show like this, honey." The pride in his voice was evident. "But she wasn't sure if she could get you accepted to the exhibit because you were under eighteen. So she decided to try to surprise you, if she could."

"Sherri," Mrs. Vey broke in, "I was fairly certain that you would be well received, and maybe even sell a few of your pieces. At worst, I knew you wouldn't be embarrassed. But I can't say I expected this."

Sherri couldn't seem to pull an intelligent response out of the whirl of her thoughts. Several long moments went by. "They're really here?" she stuttered finally. "My pictures?" For a moment she was afraid she was going to cry.

Mrs. Vey took her by the arm and steered her around. "Shall we go see?"

Sherri was glad for the time that it took them to weave their way in and out of the various galleries and partitions that had been set up. A professional exhibit! Was she dreaming? Sherri bit her lip until she tasted blood. No, she seemed to be awake.

"There," Mrs. Vey said before Sherri expected it. "There you are, see?"

Sherri moved forward slowly. She could scarcely feel her feet making contact with the floor as she saw the familiar frames and photographs grouped in a three-wall panel. There was the huge, silver-framed mat of Pharitell in all his shimmering beauty. And the closeup superimposure of Paul and Lynn James over the wide-angle shot of Rockview Ranch: the ranch buildings clustered in the foreground and the snowy peaks sparkled above the laughing couple. In the next frame, dust boiled in a rising cloud around the legs of Shane's buckskin gelding as it made a sliding, twisting turn to cut off a cow's escape. On the other side of the grouping, Terry lay stretched full length in the shade of a few aspens, hat over his face, while his horse cropped grass nearby.

On the opposite panel, Timmy stood in his Sunday suit, hands clasped behind his back, facing a tall, marble gravestone. Fresh roses lay on the grave, and a vignette of Debbie James's wedding portrait meshed softly with the clear sky. Then came a shot of Paul James riding side by side with Todd. It was a near-silhouette as their horses jogged toward the barn with the setting sun behind them. Little puffs of dust, churned up by the horses' hooves, sparkled in the slanted light. Faces were difficult to distinguish, but the postures—one very tall and one very short—were remarkably similar. Completing the trio, Kyle squatted on one heel in the dewy grass of early morning with his hand and arm outstretched to a spindly, newborn foal. The little creature, also, was extending his neck as far as possible to investigate this two-legged phenomenon.

The third panel contained more shots of the wild horses: a straight-on shot of mares and foals charging through the creek, sheets of water sparkling shoulder-high in the morning sun; a pair of yearlings rearing and striking at each other in play; a foal peeping under the belly of its coal black mother. And in the center of the grouping, the shot of Paul James, standing with Tim and Todd by the foaming jet of water at the base of Crest Spring. Cut into the center of the waterfall was the ancient, slightly scarred reproduction: an identical shot of Paul's father and grandfather.

Over near the edge of the display, on a free-standing easel, was Sherri's own portrait, the picture that she'd set up and had Kathleen take for her nearly two months before: Sherri sat on a huge, rock slab that jutted over the sheer wall at the top end of Blind Valley. The Rockies towered above her, in a cloudless sky, and the canyon fell away to nothingness below. The photo occupied an upper fourth of the mat, while script type, with a brief history of Rockview and some biographical details about Sherri, filled the rest. Fastened to the upper edge of the frame was a large, dark green rosette with gold lettering: "Honorable Mention, Northwest Photographers Association."

From a long way off, Sherri heard Mrs. Vey speak to her. "Congratulations, Sherri. You did very well."

Sherri dragged her gaze from the green rosette. Every part of her felt shaky, she realized, and her pulse was racing. She looked at her boss, then at Lynn, and then at her father. Sherri wasn't absolutely sure, but she thought she saw the glitter of tears in her dad's eyes. For some reason that she didn't understand, that did more to help her recover her composure than anything else. The cotton in her mouth seemed to vanish as she felt the need to speak to him. Uncaring of the fact that they were in public gathering, Sherri moved to her father and threw her arms around him.

"Thank you, Daddy," she said, feeling suddenly as calm as she'd ever felt in her life. "Thank you for giving me the chance to try this."

He held her tightly for a few moments before he responded. "You sure proved that you knew what you wanted to do."

"No, sir," she said, stepping back and turning to Lynn. "I didn't, really. I was praying for drawing lessons—remember?" She laughed. "But God knew what would be best." She smiled at her stepmother before giving her a hug as well.

"Sherri," Mrs. Vey spoke up. "I don't mean to bring a more mercenary note into this conversation, but there are a couple of things I need to know."

"Yes, ma'am?"

"You've had offers to buy some of the pictures. Since the Kiston show wasn't going to be a sales exhibit, I didn't know which, if any, of them you would like to sell. I just listed your entry as 'negotiable' under the sales category, and there have been several inquiries."

"Really?" Sherri was almost more surprised at this than at the original award. "Which ones?"

"There have been three offers for the picture of the stallion, one for the one of the herd, and one for the one of your brother working the cattle. It wouldn't surprise me if there were more before the end of the week. Someone was unofficially asking me about the shot of Crest Rock."

"What does it mean, though?" Sherri wasn't sure of all the ramifications. "Will I be able to print more copies for myself? Or do they buy the rights to the photos as well?"

"It depends on how you set it up," Mrs. Vey responded. "Most often, they are just buying the print. You retain all the rights on the photo. If they want to reprint it or use it somewhere else, they are responsible to make those arrangements with your permission and under your conditions. That's why I had you stamp them all as copyrighted property of the Krayfor Agency."

"Oh, well, in that case, I don't see why not." Sherri looked at her father for his approval. He nodded. "I guess we'll just leave that to you, then, unless there's something I need to do. This is your home turf." Sherri smiled as she looked at her boss.

"Yes." Mrs. Vey returned the smile. "And you don't know how glad I am that I can claim to be the one who 'discovered' you, young lady. Don't you forget that twenty years from now when they ask you where you had your start." A teasing glint showed for a moment in the lady's eyes. She patted Sherri on the arm and moved away. "Fine, then. I'm going to go carry on some business-style coversations."

Sherri, with her father and Lynn, spent the next hour wandering through the other exhibits, admiring the work of the various artists. Try as she might, Sherri couldn't keep her mind too much on any conversation. The more she looked at some of the stunning photography around her, the more ideas for future work popped into her head. She itched for a pen and a scrap of paper to start writing some of them down.

They had almost completed a full circuit of the building when Sherri heard a familiar voice speak to her father. "Paul? Hey there! How are you doing?"

"Jeff King!"

Sherri looked around in time to see her father shaking hands with Mr. King, the teacher in charge of the school publicity committee.

"It's been a while since I've had a chance to talk with you." Mr. King seemed genuinely glad to see his old classmate. Sherri's father slipped an arm around his wife and drew her forward.

"Honey, this is Jeff King. He and I went to high school together. Jeff, I don't believe you've met my wife, Lynn."

"How do you do?" Lynn extended her hand.

"Fine, thank you. Yes, I'd heard that you'd remarried, but I hadn't had the pleasure of meeting your wife until now. It's so nice to meet you, Lynn." Mr. King shook her hand and continued. "I suppose you know what your daughter has been up to with the school production?"

"She mentioned the possibilities." Sherri's father glanced sideways at her. "But I wasn't aware that anything had been decided yet."

"Well," Mr. King said with a grin, "we're working on it. She's rather convincing, but she'll have to prove that it can fit the budget. Frankly, though, I had no idea—" He made a vague gesture around with his hand, seeming to be at a loss for words. "What more can I say?" He shrugged. "This is a little above the standard for a high school junior."

"She has a lot of her mother in her." Sherri's father made the statement quietly.

Mr. King gave a perceptible start. "Of course," he responded. "She's the spitting image of Debbie, but I hadn't really thought about the artistic angle. Debbie always was a whiz—wasn't that what she wanted to study in college?"

Mr. King didn't really give anyone a chance to answer him as he hurried on in his own subject-skipping manner. "Do you know if Linda Vey is here tonight? I'd like to talk to her soon, and I thought maybe I'd run across her—"

"She's here," Sherri's father confirmed. "Sherri, she's probably over by the registration counter. Why don't you see if you can find her?"

Sherri nodded, recognizing her father's dismissal. More than likely, she figured as she made her way through the crowd, there's something he wants to ask Mr. King without me around.

Sherri hadn't covered more than half the distance to the counter, passing near to her own exhibit, when someone spoke her name. "Sherri James? Miss James?"

Sherri turned to see a red-haired stranger approaching. "Yes?"

"Miss James, my name is Harrison Rinell."

"How do you do, Mr. Rinell?" Sherri tried to copy Lynn's easy manner and her brief handshake.

"Very well, thank you. And congratulations on your placement. I believe we may have something to talk about."

"Thank you—and what might that be?"

"Miss James, are you familiar with the Pacific Photographers Club?"

"No, sir. I'm afraid I'm not."

"Well, that's not surprising. We're not an extremely large organization, and we are located in California. But I saw your exhibit here just this evening. It's very well done."

"Thank you."

"Frankly, I hadn't come across your name before, but when I read the bio' on your portrait and realized you are a high school student, I wondered if you were aware of our college scholarship program."

As Sherri shook her head, he hurried on. "It's a fairly recent development for us, but it's becoming quite popular among our members. They really like to 'support' the profession—and hobby—that they love so much. Our choices are made strictly on the basis of the potential that we judge, but I daresay you'd have a good chance if you were interested in applying."

Sherri wasn't sure she should believe him. "I take it you're serious?" Her words were half-question, half-statement.

"Quite." The man's smile grew broader.

"And for what particular school are these scholarships?" Sherri said, silently adding, Left Wing Academy of America?

"That would be your choice, of course. It strikes me that a young lady of your poise and talent would have an excellent school already in mind."

Your poise and talent? Sherri gritted her teeth to hold back a whoop of laughter. Who did he think he was talking about? Or was he just trying to impress her with his vocabulary? She gave herself a mental shake, though, reminding herself of the difference in his perspective from hers. He'd never seen her anywhere but here—could it possibly be that she was beginning to gain some ground after all?

Unexpectedly, her eye was caught by a flash of light in the frame of Debbie James's photograph. Sherri turned slightly to look. A long moment passed, and her thoughts were swept away from the stranger. This would have pleased her, Sherri thought. It probably does please her—surely she knows. It was through her that the Lord gave me an interest and an ability in art in the first place.

And who continued to make it possible for you? The now-familiar little voice reminded her. Who played the biggest part in giving you the chance you never thought you could have? Who pushed you when you fought it? Who was patient when you were impossible, believed in you when you mistrusted her, and loved you when you hated her? The thoughts weren't new, but Sherri felt them with a special clarity as her gaze dropped to the face of Lynn in the portrait below.

Now there's "poise and talent," she thought. And every bit of it is nothing but a concentration that's on others and off herself. If I could ever begin to be to others what she's been to me. . . . Sherri smiled as the familiar verse spoke out from her memory: *Every good gift and every perfect gift is from above, and cometh down from the Father of lights, with whom is no variableness, neither shadow of turning.*

Sherri dragged her attention back to Mr. Rinell, aware that he was still waiting for an answer. But as she did so, she saw Lynn approaching them. "Yes, I do have a school in mind, sir. But if I can change the subject for a minute, there's someone here you need to meet."

They both turned to Lynn as she came near and spoke. "Sherri? We found Mrs. Vey back there, so I came to make sure that you weren't still looking for her." Lynn smiled at them both. "Are you making new friends?"

"Yes, I am. This is Harrison Rinell, of the Pacific Photographers Club." Sherri slipped an arm around Lynn as she spoke. "Mr. Rinell, this," she paused slightly for emphasis, "is my mother."